THE
Vegan
Bread Machine
COOKBOOK

THE
Vegan
Bread Machine

 COOKBOOK

Splendid Plant-Based and Dairy-Free Vegan Breads

SHANE MARTIN

HARVARD COMMON PRESS

Quarto.com

© 2025 Quarto Publishing Group USA Inc.
Text © 2025 Shane Martin

First Published in 2025 by Harvard Common Press, an imprint of The Quarto Group,
100 Cummings Center, Suite 265-D, Beverly, MA 01915, USA.
T (978) 282-9590 F (978) 283-2742

Harvard Common Press titles are also available at discount for retail, wholesale, promotional, and bulk purchase. For details, contact the Special Sales Manager by email at specialsales@quarto.com or by mail at The Quarto Group, Attn: Special Sales Manager, 100 Cummings Center, Suite 265-D, Beverly, MA 01915, USA.

29 28 27 26 25   1 2 3 4 5

ISBN: 978-0-7603-9271-3

Digital edition published in 2025
eISBN: 978-0-7603-9272-0

Library of Congress Cataloging-in-Publication Data available

Design: John Clifford
Page Layout: John Clifford and Tim Littleton
Photography: Shane Martin except pages 8–10, 13, 19, 21, 70, 73, 79, 89, 91, 92, 103, 111, 112, 114, 134, 143, 146, 148, 152 are Shutterstock

Printed in China

To my beloved Andrea, my soulmate and best friend.
For twenty-five wonderful years, your unconditional
love, constant support, and shining spirit have been
my guiding light. You are the steady anchor that
enables me to dream big dreams yet brings me back
down to earth when I need it. If I had every word
and a thousand years to use them, that still would
not be enough to say all that you are to me.
I love you,
Shane.

Contents

Introduction

The Joys of Vegan Bread Machine Baking: Keeping It Simple, Delicious, and Plant-Based

Hey there, fellow plant-powered pals! Are you ready to revolutionize your bread game with the magic of vegan baking? Well, buckle up, because we're about to embark on a flavor-packed journey with none other than me, Shane Martin, bread machine edition!

Imagine waking up to the aroma of freshly baked bread wafting through your kitchen, without even lifting a finger. Yup, that's the power of the bread machine! And, I'm here to show you how to harness that power to create mouthwatering, plant-based loaves that will have you coming back for seconds (and thirds).

Now, you might be thinking, "But wait, can a bread machine really handle vegan recipes?" Oh, ye of little faith! Believe me, your trusty bread machine is more than up to the task. In fact, it's about to become your new best friend in the kitchen.

Look, I'm all about keeping things easy-peasy (bread)squeezy. Who needs complicated kneading techniques or hours of rising time when you've got a bread machine on your side? With just the push of a few buttons, you'll be well on your way to fluffy, golden-brown perfection.

So, what's the secret to our vegan bread machine success? Hint: It's not unicorn tears or fairy dust. (Although, I admit that would be cool.) Nope, it's all about choosing the right ingredients and letting your bread machine do the heavy lifting. Think hearty whole grains, nutty flours, and a whole lot of plant-based goodness.

But let's address the elephant in the room: I get it—baking bread can be intimidating, especially if you're used to store-bought loaves. Will your dough rise? Will your crust be crispy? Will your friends secretly conspire to steal your bread machine? Take a deep breath and repeat after me: "I've got this!" Trust me, with a little bit of patience and a whole lot of trial and error, you'll be churning out bakery-worthy loaves in no time.

And hey, even if your first attempt at vegan bread machine baking leaves something to be desired, give yourself a pat on the back for trying! Rome wasn't built in a day, and neither was your bread machine empire. Plus, there's no such thing as a bread mishap when it comes to taste testing, am I right?

So, whether you're a seasoned pro or a bread machine newbie, dust off that machine, load up your ingredients, and get ready to elevate your bread game to new heights! Because I'm all about spreading the joy of vegan bread machine baking—one delicious slice at a time. Happy baking, friends!

UNDERSTANDING YOUR BREAD MACHINE

Understanding your bread machine is essential for mastering the art of breadmaking at home. Each bread machine comes with its own set of features and functions, which may vary from model to model. Familiarizing yourself with these features, such as crust settings, loaf size options, and various bread types, allows you to customize your baking experience according to your preferences.

Additionally, understanding the timing and sequence of the breadmaking process, from kneading to rising and baking, empowers you to troubleshoot any issues that may arise and ensures consistently delicious results with every loaf. By delving into the intricacies of your bread machine, you unlock a world of possibilities, enabling you to experiment with different recipes, ingredients, and techniques to create homemade bread that suits your taste perfectly.

Getting to Know Your Appliance

Familiarize yourself with the different settings and features of your bread machine, including the various bread cycles (such as basic, whole-wheat, gluten-free, etc.). Also take the time to read up on the crust settings and delay timer options.

Take the time to read the instruction manual thoroughly. It's important to understand how to properly operate and care for your bread machine.

Experiment with different loaf sizes to see what works best for your needs. If you're baking for a small family, start with smaller loaves. If you are baking for a larger group or gathering, or if you eat bread often, try the larger loaf sizes.

Bread machines vary, so be sure to get to know the capacity of your machine. Avoid overfilling it, as this can lead to uneven baking and poor results.

Explore additional features your bread machine may have, such as a fruit and nut dispenser or a programmable memory function. Learn how to use them effectively to enhance your bread-making experience.

Tips for Optimal Results

Use fresh, high-quality ingredients for the best-tasting bread. This includes fresh flour, active yeast, and any additional add-ins such as nuts, seeds, or dried fruits.

Measure your ingredients accurately, using either a kitchen scale or measuring cups designed for dry and liquid ingredients.

Follow the recipe instructions carefully, including the order in which ingredients should be added to the bread machine pan.

Make sure your ingredients are at room temperature before adding them to the bread machine, as this will help ensure proper yeast activation and more even baking.

Regularly clean and maintain your bread machine according to the manufacturer's instructions. Keep it in good working condition to prevent any issues from arising.

Troubleshooting Common Issues

If your bread isn't rising properly, check your yeast. The freshness of yeast makes a difference; make sure yours has not expired. Also, ensure that you're using the correct type of yeast for your recipe (e.g., instant yeast, active dry yeast).

If your bread is coming out too dense or heavy, try using less flour or increasing the amount of liquid in the recipe. You can also try adding a little bit of vital wheat gluten to help improve the bread's texture and rise.

If your bread is burning on the outside but still undercooked on the inside, try reducing the baking temperature or covering the bread with aluminum foil halfway through the baking process to prevent over-browning.

If your bread machine is making unusual noises or not functioning properly, check for any obstructions or loose parts. Clean the machine thoroughly. If the issue persists, consult the instruction manual for troubleshooting tips or contact the manufacturer for assistance.

ESSENTIAL INGREDIENTS

Starting with top-notch ingredients is crucial for crafting high-quality bread, making it worthwhile to prioritize investing in the finest essentials within your budget. Below is a list of pantry staples that are essential for preparing homemade bread that you'll cherish.

Remember, creating your own bread is not just about nourishing your body. It is also about feeding your soul. Embrace the process with enthusiasm and creativity. Experiment with different flavors, textures, and techniques to tailor your bread exactly to your liking. With each loaf, you're not just baking bread; you're crafting a masterpiece that reflects your passion and dedication.

So, gather your ingredients, roll up your sleeves, and let the aroma of freshly baked bread fill your home with warmth and joy. Your journey to becoming a breadmaking aficionado begins now!

Flour Varieties and Their Uses

Organic Unbleached All-Purpose Flour: This is a versatile flour that works well for most bread machine recipes. It has a moderate protein content and produces a soft, tender crumb.

Ah, the illustrious organic wheat flour! Why settle for anything less than wheat that's been pampered with pesticide-free affection and nurtured in fields where even the bugs are on a first-name basis with the farmers? Sure, you could opt for the regular stuff and risk ingesting a cocktail of chemicals with your morning toast, but where's the fun in that? Organic wheat flour not only boasts a cleaner conscience but also promises a taste so pure, it'll make your taste buds do a little happy dance. Plus, think of the bragging rights you'll have when you casually mention your organic sourdough at brunch. So, go ahead, embrace the organic craze, and let your flour sack be the envy of all the other grains in the pantry!

Whole-Wheat Flour: Made from the entire wheat kernel, whole-wheat flour adds nutritional value and a hearty flavor to bread. It can be used on its own or mixed with all-purpose flour for a lighter texture.

Bread Flour: With a higher protein content than all-purpose flour, bread flour is ideal for making yeast bread as it provides better gluten development and a chewier texture.

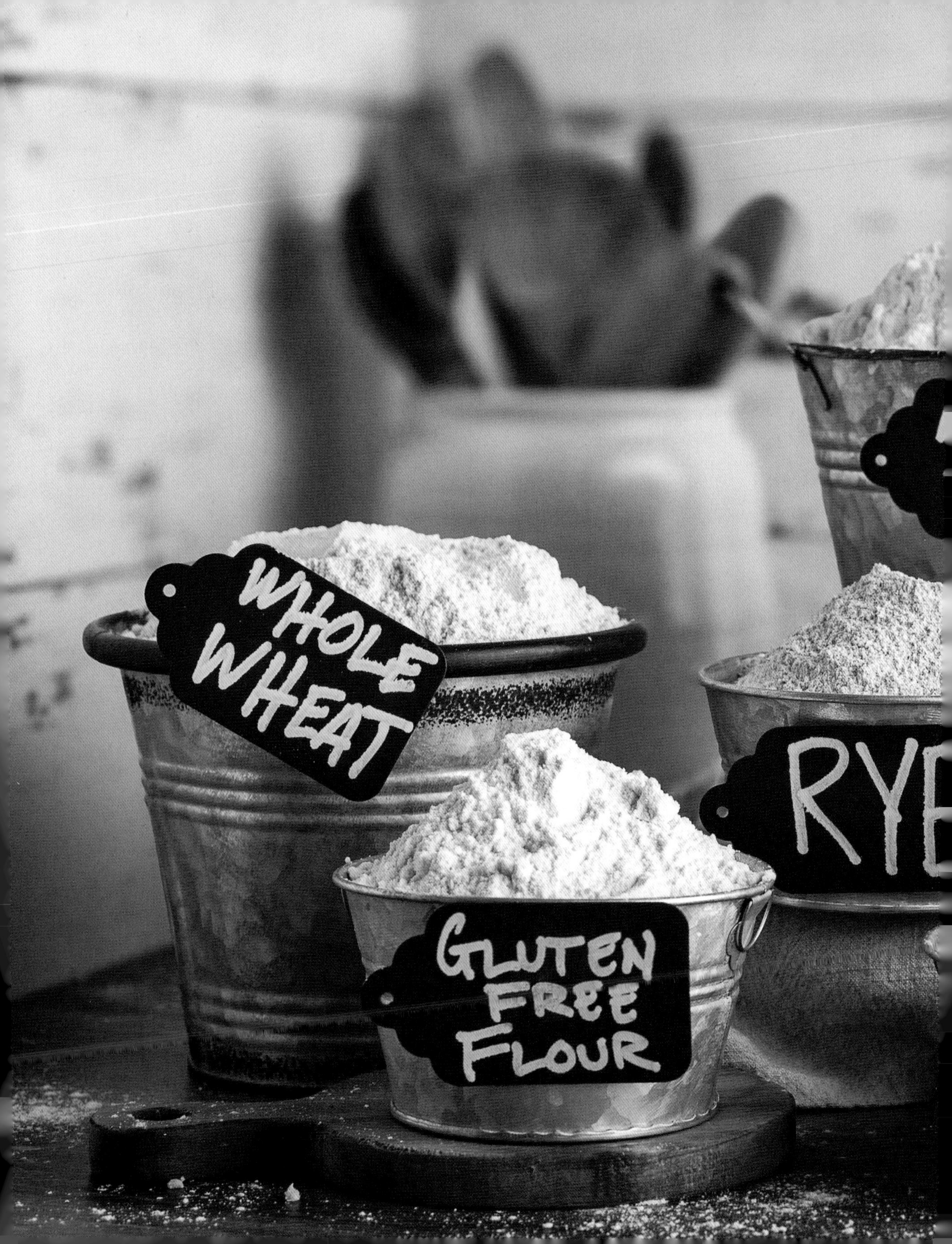
WHOLE WHEAT
GLUTEN FREE FLOUR
RYE

Gluten-Free Flour: These flours can be tricky, but I've tried to make it as simple as possible. *Do not use almond flour!* Be sure to use either 1:1 gluten-free flour or gluten-free bread flour. These recipes are suitable for individuals with gluten sensitivities or allergies. When using gluten-free flours, it may be necessary to use binders such as xanthan gum or guar gum to help the bread rise and hold its shape.

Spelt Flour: Spelt flour is an ancient-grain flour with a nutty flavor. It can be used in place of wheat flour for a bread that is a little more dense and that has a stronger flavor.

Plant-Based Binders and Leavening Agents

Yeast: Yeast is a crucial leavening agent in breadmaking, responsible for causing the dough to rise. There are different types of yeast available, including active dry yeast, instant yeast, and fresh yeast. When it comes to the bread machine, veering off the ingredient list is like taking a detour through a maze of gluten-filled chaos. Sure, you could toss in a handful of raisins or sprinkle some oregano for good measure, but beware the wrath of the yeast gods! Stick to the script, my friend, and your bread will rise to golden perfection. Stray too far, and you might end up with a loaf that's more Frankenstein's monster than fluffy carb delight.

Baking Powder and Baking Soda: These chemical leavening agents react with moisture and acidic ingredients to produce carbon dioxide gas, which helps the bread rise. Baking powder is typically used in recipes that do not contain acidic ingredients, while baking soda requires an acidic component, such as vinegar or lemon juice, to activate.

Flaxseed Meal and Chia Seeds: These plant-based ingredients can be used as binders in vegan baking. When mixed with water, they form a gel-like consistency that helps hold the ingredients together in the absence of eggs.

Enhancing Flavors with Herbs and Spices

Rosemary: This aromatic herb adds a savory flavor to bread. It pairs well with olive oil and garlic. Try my Rosemary and Olive French Bread (page 49) or the Cranberry Pecan Rosemary Bread (page 75).

Cinnamon: A warm and comforting spice, cinnamon adds sweetness and depth of flavor to bread, especially when combined with ingredients such as raisins or applesauce. This book includes recipes for Cinnamon Swirl Bread (page 132), Easy-to-Make Cinnamon Rolls (page 107), and even a gluten-free option (page 88).

Garlic Powder: For savory bread recipes, garlic powder can add a punch of flavor without the hassle of mincing fresh garlic. If you are a garlic lover, be sure to check out the Vegan Parmesan Garlic Bread (page 74), Vegan Buttery Garlic-Herb Knots (page 110), and the Garlic Pull-Apart Bubble Loaf (page 81). They are all worth that extra effort.

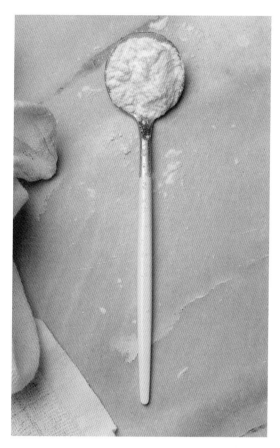

Nutritional Yeast: Often used in vegan cooking to add a cheesy flavor, nutritional yeast can enhance the savory profile of bread and make it more flavorful. Nutritional yeast is great on breadsticks (page 109) and/or used in the Easy Tomato-Basil Bread Machine Bread (page 69).

Turmeric: This golden spice not only adds color to bread but also offers anti-inflammatory properties and a subtle earthy flavor.

By understanding the characteristics and uses of different flour varieties, plant-based binders, leavening agents, herbs, and spices, you can create a diverse range of delicious vegan breads in your bread machine.

Aquafaba

Aquafaba, the magical liquid from canned chickpeas, serves as a versatile egg substitute in eggless baking recipes for bread. Its unique protein and starch content mimics the binding and leavening properties of eggs, resulting in fluffy and moist loaves without the need for animal products. So next time you're whipping up a batch of vegan bread, don't toss that chickpea water—let it work its wonders in your dough!

Flax Eggs

In vegan baking, flax eggs serve as a reliable substitute for traditional eggs, providing binding and moisture to your recipes. Simply mix 1 tablespoon (7 g) of ground flaxseed with 2½ tablespoons (38 ml) of warm water in a small bowl. Let it sit for about 10 minutes until it thickens, resembling the consistency of a regular egg. This flax egg concoction works wonders in muffins, cookies, and even bread, ensuring your vegan creations rise to delicious perfection. Try it in the Easy-to-Make Cinnamon Rolls on page 107 and the Big Bear Claws from the Bread Machine on page 136.

Xanthan Gum and Gluten-Free Baking

Ah, xanthan gum, the gluten-free baker's secret weapon against culinary chaos! This magical powder, essentially derived from fermented sugar, acts as a trusty sidekick in gluten-free baking, swooping in to save your recipes from crumbling into sad little heaps. With just a pinch of xanthan gum, your gluten-free goodies transform into masterpieces of structural integrity, defying gravity and mocking the very notion of gluten's dominance in the baking world. So, fear not, intrepid baker, for with xanthan gum in your arsenal, you shall conquer the realm of gluten-free delights with ease and flair!

A WORD ABOUT LOAF SIZES

When using a 2-pound (908-g) bread machine, it's important to note that some recipes in this cookbook may yield smaller loaves. Fear not, faithful baker, and stick to the recipes provided! If your bread machine doesn't accommodate 2-pound loaves, fret not; simply employ a recipe converter to adjust your ingredient amounts. These converters are as abundant as grains of flour on a baker's apron and can be easily accessed online, ensuring your breadmaking adventures remain seamless and delightful.

1

DAILY LOAVES

Warm, fresh bread is one of life's simple pleasures—the aroma wafting through the kitchen, the crusty exterior giving way to a soft, fluffy interior. This chapter covers classic everyday loaves like basic white, wholesome wheat, and rustic rye. Master these foundational recipes and you'll have delicious vegan bread at your fingertips daily with minimal effort. Get ready to fill your home with the comforting scent and taste of homemade bread.

Basic White Bread

Indulge in the delight of this vegan white bread recipe. It has an irresistible pillowy soft interior and golden crust. Your kitchen will be filled with the tantalizing aroma of freshly baked goodness.

INGREDIENTS

1½ cups (355 ml) water, lukewarm

3 tablespoons (42 g) vegan butter, room temperature, cut into ½-inch (1-cm) pieces

1 tablespoon (13 g) organic cane sugar

1½ teaspoons kosher salt

4 cups (500 g) organic unbleached all-purpose flour

¼ cup (60 ml) unsweetened oat milk or nondairy milk of your choice, lukewarm

1½ teaspoons instant, active dry, or bread machine yeast

DIRECTIONS

1. Be sure the kneading paddle is attached to your bread machine pan. Add the water, vegan butter, sugar, salt, flour, nondairy milk, and yeast to the bread pan in the order listed.

2. Select the Basic or White setting. Then choose the desired crust color (if that's an option on your machine), and select the size (2-pound [907-g] loaf). Press start.

3. Once the bread has finished baking, turn the bread out onto a wire rack to cool. Slice and enjoy.

Makes one 2-pound (907-g) loaf

Easy Oat Bread

This amazing, healthy, and wholesome oatmeal bread recipe brings deliciousness to any lunch box. With a subtle flavor profile and no overpowering spices, it serves as a versatile base for a wide range of lunch sandwiches—from vegan chicken salad to the faithful PB & J.

INGREDIENTS

1¼ cups (295 ml) unsweetened soymilk, lukewarm

2½ tablespoons (35 g) vegan butter, room temperature, cut into ½-inch (1-cm) pieces

2 tablespoons (40 g) pure maple syrup

1¼ teaspoons kosher salt

3¾ cups (469 g) organic unbleached all-purpose flour

1 cup (96 g) old-fashioned rolled oats

2¼ teaspoons (9 g) instant, active dry, or bread machine yeast

DIRECTIONS

1. Be sure the kneading paddle is attached to your bread machine pan. Add the soymilk, vegan butter, maple syrup, salt, flour, oats, and yeast to the bread pan in the order listed.

2. Select the White setting on the bread machine. Select the desired crust color (if available), and choose the loaf size (2 pound [907 g]). Press start.

3. Once the bread has finished baking, remove it from the pan. Place it on a wire rack to cool. Allow the bread to cool completely before slicing.

Makes one 2-pound (907-g) loaf

Milk and Maple Bread

Both kids and grown-ups enjoy the pillowy softness and subtle sweetness of this comfort-food bread. The flavor of maple makes it an ideal choice for morning toast or a cozy afternoon snack.

INGREDIENTS

1 cup plus 1 tablespoon (250 ml) unsweetened almond milk, lukewarm

3 tablespoons (60 g) pure maple syrup

3 tablespoons (42 g) vegan butter, melted

3 cups (360 g) white bread flour

1½ teaspoons kosher salt

2 teaspoons (8 g) instant, active dry, or bread machine yeast

DIRECTIONS

1. Be sure the kneading paddle is attached to your bread machine pan. Add the nondairy milk, maple syrup, vegan butter, flour, salt, and yeast to the bread pan in the order listed.

2. Select the Basic or White setting. Choose medium crust color (if available), and select the 2-pound (907-g) loaf size. Press start.

3. Once the bread is finished, remove it from the pan. Transfer it to a wire rack to completely cool before slicing.

Makes one 2-pound (907-g) loaf

Classic Rye Bread

Enjoy the wholesome goodness of this vegan rye bread. This loaf is characterized by its simplicity and basic ingredients, making it a delightful choice for those who appreciate straightforward and cruelty-free baking. This is a delightful concoction that defies the laws of tradition with every eggless, dairy-less slice! As it kneads and rises in the confines of your bread machine, it whispers tales of rebellion against the status quo of traditional baking. So gather your ingredients, summon your bread machine, and let this loaf of plant-powered audacity be the star of your next sandwich extravaganza!

INGREDIENTS

1⅔ cups (395 ml) water, lukewarm

1¼ teaspoons kosher salt

3 cups (375 g) organic unbleached all-purpose flour

2 cups (212 g) rye flour

1 tablespoon (12 g) instant, active dry, or bread machine yeast

DIRECTIONS

1. Be sure the kneading paddle is attached to your bread machine pan. Add the water, salt, flours, and yeast to the bread pan in the order listed.

2. Select the Basic or White setting. Choose the desired crust color (if available); I prefer medium. Select the loaf size (2 pound [907 g]). Press start.

3. Once the bread has finished baking, remove it from the pan. Transfer the bread to a wire rack, and let it cool completely before slicing.

Makes one 2-pound (907-g) loaf

Basic Bread Machine French Bread Loaf

In North America, people are often surprised that the French eat breads made in a familiar loaf shape, as opposed to elongated baguettes. But in fact they do, and not infrequently. With its golden, crusty exterior and soft, airy interior, this plant-based delight captures the essence of a traditional French bread in a convenient and versatile sandwich-loaf shape.

INGREDIENTS

1½ cups (355 ml) water, lukewarm

1½ teaspoons kosher salt

4 cups (500 g) organic unbleached all-purpose flour

1½ teaspoons instant, active dry, or bread machine yeast

DIRECTIONS

1. Be sure the kneading paddle is attached to your bread machine pan. Add the water, salt, flour, and yeast to the bread pan in the order listed.

2. If your bread machine comes with a French setting, choose that; otherwise, select the Basic or White setting. Choose the desired crust color (if available) and the 2-pound (907-g) loaf size. Press start.

3. When the bread is finished baking, remove it from the pan. Place it on a wire rack, and allow it to completely cool before slicing.

Makes one 2-pound (907-g) loaf

Breakfast Cereal Bread

Behold, the breakfast cereal bread. This vegan delight boasts a hearty blend of grains, providing a flavorful and nourishing experience. It's an ingenious fusion of morning sustenance and breadmaking brilliance! With crunchy nuggets of breakfast delight nestled within each slice, it's like having your cereal and eating it too. Whether you're munching on it with your morning coffee or sneaking a slice in the dead of night, this bread will have you rethinking the boundaries of breakfast bliss.

INGREDIENTS

1¼ cups (295 ml) water, lukewarm

⅓ cup (77 g) unsweetened plain vegan yogurt

¼ cup (55 g) vegan butter, room temperature, cut into ½-inch (1-cm) pieces

2 tablespoons (30 g) packed light or dark brown sugar

1½ teaspoons kosher salt

2 cups (250 g) whole-wheat flour

2 cups (250 g) organic unbleached all-purpose flour

2⅔ cups (weight varies) your favorite multigrain cereal (e.g., Total, Bran Flakes, Uncle Sam)

2½ teaspoons (10 g) instant, active dry, or bread machine yeast

DIRECTIONS

1. Make sure the kneading paddle is attached to the pan. Add the water, vegan yogurt, vegan butter, brown sugar, salt, flours, cereal, and yeast to the bread pan in the order listed.

2. Select the Whole Wheat setting (if available). If not, use the Basic or White setting. Choose the desired crust color (if available), and select the 2-pound (907-g) loaf size. Press start.

3. Once the bread is finished, remove it from the bread pan. Place it on a wire rack, and let it cool before slicing.

Makes one 2-pound (907-g) loaf

"Nuts Over You" Whole-Wheat Bread

This bread is tailored to your tastes because it leaves the choice of nuts and seeds up to you. You can pick any ones you like, either alone or in combination. My favorite is a combination of walnuts and sunflower seeds, in about a 2:1 ratio of the nuts to the seeds.

INGREDIENTS

1 cup plus 2 tablespoons (263 ml) unsweetened almond milk, lukewarm

2 tablespoons (28 ml) apple cider vinegar

1 teaspoon kosher salt

1½ tablespoons (21 g) vegan butter, room temperature, cut into ½-inch (1-cm) pieces

1½ tablespoons (14 g) pure maple syrup

2¼ cups (282 g) whole-wheat flour

1¼ cups (157 g) organic unbleached all-purpose flour

1 tablespoon (12 g) instant, active dry, or bread machine yeast

¾ cup (weight varies) nuts and seeds, such as pecans, walnuts, sunflower seeds, or chia seeds

DIRECTIONS

1. Make sure the kneading paddle is attached to the pan. Whisk together the almond milk and apple cider vinegar in a small bowl until small bubbles form on top to make vegan buttermilk. Pour the buttermilk into the bread pan.

2. Add the salt, vegan butter, maple syrup, flours, and yeast to the bread pan in the order listed. Select the Whole Wheat setting (if available). If not, use the Basic or White setting. Choose the desired crust color (if available) and the 2-pound (907-g) loaf size. Press start.

3. When the Add-In signal sounds, toss in the nuts and seeds.

4. Once the cycle has finished, remove the bread from the machine. Allow it to cool completely on a wire rack before slicing.

Makes one 2-pound (907-g) loaf

Wheat Bran and Molasses Bread

Molasses, a centuries-old ingredient, is making a welcome comeback as an alternative to processed white sugars. Combining it with the wheat bran and oats yields a bread that is at once healthy and sweet. This wheat bran and molasses bread isn't just any loaf—it's a delicious throwback to a time when sugar wasn't afraid to show its true colors. With each bite, you'll feel like you're channeling your inner pioneer, bravely navigating the treacherous seas of modern dietary fads. So, raise a toast to molasses, the unsung hero of sweeteners, and enjoy this hearty bread that's as wholesome as it is flavorful.

INGREDIENTS

1½ cups (355 ml) water, lukewarm

1¼ teaspoons kosher salt

1½ tablespoons (21 g) vegan butter, softened, cut into ½-inch (1-cm) pieces

2 tablespoons (40 g) molasses

2¼ cups (282 g) whole-wheat flour

1½ cups (188 g) organic unbleached all-purpose flour

½ cup plus 2 tablespoons (60 g) old-fashioned rolled oats (not quick cooking)

⅓ cup plus 2 tablespoons (46 g) wheat bran

1 tablespoon (12 g) instant, active dry, or bread machine yeast

DIRECTIONS

1. Fit the kneading paddle into the bread pan. Add the water, salt, vegan butter, molasses, flours, oats, wheat bran, and yeast to the bread pan in the order listed.

2. Choose the Whole Wheat setting (if available). If not, use the Basic or White setting. Select the desired crust color (if available) and the 2-pound (907-g) loaf size. Press start.

3. Once the baking is complete, transfer the bread to a wire rack. Let it cool completely before slicing.

Makes one 2-pound (907-g) loaf

Seeded Whole-Grain Loaf

This is a powerhouse of nutrition disguised as a delectable slice of bread! Packed with flaxseeds, it's not just your average loaf; it's a superhero in the world of plant-based diets, swooping in to deliver those elusive omega-3 fatty acids with a side of protein and fiber. So, brace yourself for a guilt-free indulgence that'll have you feeling like a health guru with every bite.

INGREDIENTS

1⅓ cups (315 ml) unsweetened almond milk, lukewarm

3 tablespoons (60 g) pure maple syrup

2 tablespoons (30 ml) extra-virgin olive oil

1¼ teaspoons kosher salt

2⅔ cups (333 g) whole-wheat flour

2 tablespoons (12 g) old-fashioned rolled oats

4 teaspoons (9 g) vital wheat gluten

1 tablespoon (13 g) millet

1 tablespoon (9 g) sunflower seeds

2 tablespoons (24 g) flaxseed meal

2¼ teaspoons (9 g) instant, active dry, or bread machine yeast

DIRECTIONS

1. Be sure the kneading paddle is attached to your bread machine pan. Add the nondairy milk, maple syrup, olive oil, salt, flour, oats, gluten, millet, sunflower seeds, flax, and yeast to the bread pan in the order listed.

2. Select the Basic or White setting. Choose the desired crust color (if available) and the 2-pound (907-g) loaf size. Press start.

3. Check the dough after 5 minutes of mixing. Add 1 to 2 tablespoons of water or flour if needed.

4. Once the baking has finished, remove the bread from the bread pan. Transfer it to a wire rack, and let it cool completely before slicing.

Makes one 2-pound (907-g) loaf

Healthy Whole-Wheat Bread

This is a sweet loaf of golden whole-wheat bread that's slightly firm but still tender inside. It's excellent for toast and sandwiches, and it's what I use for making vegan croutons.

INGREDIENTS

1¼ cups (295 ml) water, lukewarm

1¼ teaspoons kosher salt

2½ tablespoons (35 g) vegan butter, room temperature, cut into ½-inch (1-cm) pieces

2 tablespoons (26 g) organic cane sugar

2½ cups (300 g) whole-wheat flour

1½ cups (188 g) organic unbleached all-purpose flour

2 tablespoons (13 g) rye flour

1 tablespoon (12 g) instant, active dry, or bread machine yeast

DIRECTIONS

1. Make sure the kneading paddle is attached to the bread pan. Add the water, salt, vegan butter, sugar, flours, and yeast to the bread pan in the order listed.

2. Select the Whole Wheat setting (if available). If not, use the Basic or White setting. Choose the desired crust color (if available) and the 2-pound (907-g) loaf size. Press start.

3. Once the bread is ready, take it out of the machine. Transfer it from the pan to a wire rack. Once the bread is completely cool, slice and enjoy!

Makes one 2-pound (907-g) loaf

Whole-Wheat Cornmeal Bread

If you're looking for the perfect piece of toast for breakfast or sandwiches, this is it! The texture of the cornmeal and subtle sweetness of brown sugar make this bread simply irresistible.

INGREDIENTS

1⅓ cups (315 ml) water, room temperature

2 tablespoons (30 g) packed light brown sugar

¼ cup (60 ml) aquafaba (see page 20)

2 tablespoons (28 g) vegan butter, room temperature, cut into ½-inch (1-cm) pieces

1½ teaspoons kosher salt

¾ cup (105 g) cornmeal

¾ cup (94 g) whole-wheat flour

2¾ cups (340 g) white bread flour

2½ teaspoons (10 g) instant, active dry, or bread machine yeast

DIRECTIONS

1. Be sure the kneading paddle is attached to your bread machine pan. Add water, brown sugar, aquafaba, vegan butter, salt, cornmeal, flours, and yeast to the bread pan in the order listed.

2. Select the Basic or White setting. Select medium crust color (if available), and choose the 2-pound (907-g) loaf size. Press start.

3. Once the bread is finished, remove it from the bread pan. Transfer it to a wire rack, and let it cool completely before slicing.

Makes one 2-pound (907-g) loaf

English Muffin Bread

You are going to love this English muffin bread! It has the distinct taste and texture of traditional English muffins in a loaf of bread. It is characterized by a soft and spongy interior with a slightly chewy crust, making it ideal for toasting and serving with butter or jam.

INGREDIENTS

1 teaspoon apple cider vinegar

¼–⅓ cup (60–80 ml) water

1 cup (235 ml) unsweetened almond milk, lukewarm

2 tablespoons (28 g) vegan butter, room temperature, cut into ½-inch (1-cm) pieces

1½ teaspoons kosher salt

1½ teaspoons organic cane sugar

½ teaspoon baking powder

3½ cups (439 g) organic unbleached all-purpose flour

2¼ teaspoons (9 g) instant, active dry, or bread machine yeast

DIRECTIONS

1. Be sure the kneading paddle is attached to your bread machine pan. When you add the flour, be sure to measure it carefully or spoon it gently into a cup, then sweep off any excess. During the summer or humid conditions, use the smaller amount of water; in winter or dry climates, use the larger amount.

2. Add the vinegar, water, nondairy milk, vegan butter, salt, sugar, baking powder, flour, and yeast to the bread pan in the order listed.

3. Select the Basic or White setting. Choose the light crust option (if available) and the 2-pound (907-g) loaf size. Around the midpoint of the second kneading cycle, check the dough; it should be soft, smooth, and slightly sticky. Adjust the consistency with additional flour or water, if needed.

4. For an authentic English muffin effect, take out the dough either after the final kneading or before the final rise and roll it in cornmeal.

5. Place the dough back in the machine for rising and baking.

6. Once the bread is finished, remove it from the machine. Let it cool on a wire rack before slicing.

Makes one 2-pound (907-g) loaf

2

EUROPEAN AND ARTISAN BREADS

Take your bread machine skills to the next level with the rustic, crusty loaves found in European bakeries. This chapter explores the time-honored techniques and flavors of French baguettes, Italian ciabatta, and other artisan favorites. Learn to achieve that perfect crackling crust and light, airy interior with simple ingredients and your trusty bread machine. Bring the taste of the Old World straight to your kitchen.

Easy Rustic Italian Loaf

If you can afford it, use a good variety of olive oil in this recipe. The olive oil helps give the bread an Italian flavor and charm. Introducing vegan bread machine Italian bread—because who needs eggs and dairy when you've got the Mediterranean sun and a dash of Italian flair? This loaf is a culinary masterpiece that'll transport you straight to the cobblestone streets of Rome, minus the jet lag. So, let your bread machine do the kneading while you practice your best Italian gestures, because this loaf is about to steal the spotlight at your next carb-filled extravaganza!

INGREDIENTS

1½ cups (355 ml) water, lukewarm

2 tablespoons (30 ml) extra-virgin olive oil

1 teaspoon kosher salt

1½ teaspoons organic cane sugar

4 cups (500 g) organic unbleached all-purpose flour

½ cup (50 g) wheat bran (I like Bob's Red Mill.)

1½ teaspoons instant, active dry, or bread machine yeast

DIRECTIONS

1. Be sure the kneading paddle is attached the bread machine pan. Add the water, olive oil, salt, sugar, flour, wheat bran, and yeast to the bread pan in the order listed.

2. If your bread machine comes with a French setting, choose that; otherwise, select the Basic or White setting. Choose the desired crust color (if available), and select the 2-pound (907-g) loaf size. Press start.

3. Once the bread is finished, remove it from the pan. Allow it to completely cool on a wire rack before you slice it.

Makes one 2-pound (907-g) loaf

Vegan Herb and Parmesan Focaccia

I make this focaccia when we have company and we want to serve something fancy. I don't tell them how little work went into it!

INGREDIENTS

FOR THE DOUGH

1 cup plus 2 tablespoons (263 ml) water, lukewarm

2½ tablespoons (38 ml) extra-virgin olive oil, plus more for the pan

1 tablespoon (3 g) Italian seasoning

1½ teaspoons kosher salt

3 cups plus 3 tablespoons (383 g) white bread flour

1½ teaspoons instant, active dry, or bread machine yeast

Cornmeal, for dusting

FOR THE TOPPING

3 tablespoons (45 ml) extra-virgin olive oil

⅓ cup (40 g) vegan parmesan cheese (see note)

¾ teaspoon kosher salt

¼ cup (12 g) Italian seasoning

DIRECTIONS

1. Attach the kneading paddle to the bread machine pan. Add the water, olive oil, Italian seasoning, salt, flour, and yeast to the bread pan in the order listed.

2. Select the Dough setting. Press start.

3. Once the cycle completes, lightly flour a work surface. Transfer the dough to the floured surface. Press down in the middle of the dough to expel air, then allow it to rest for at least 10 minutes.

4. Prepare a shallow rimmed baking pan by brushing it with olive oil and lightly sprinkling with cornmeal. After the dough has finished resting, roll it out to the desired size and place it in the prepared pan.

5. Loosely cover the pan with plastic wrap. Let the dough rise in a warm spot for 1 hour, or until it doubles in size.

6. Preheat your oven to 450°F (230°C). While the oven preheats, remove the plastic wrap from the dough and begin assembling your focaccia with the topping ingredients. Oil your fingers and press into the focaccia, creating small craters. Drizzle with olive oil and evenly sprinkle with vegan parmesan, salt, and Italian seasoning.

7. Bake for 25 minutes, or until the focaccia is deeply golden and puffy with a crisp crust.

Makes 1 large loaf

Note: Use grated vegan parmesan if available. If not, buy shredded and pulse it in a blender or food processor to achieve a finer consistency. I like Follow Your Heart brand parmesan.

Rosemary and Olive French Bread

As a general rule, if you use green olives in this bread it will have a tarter and more assertive olive flavor—which suits some people's tastes but not others. If there are kids in your house, or you simply want a milder flavor, lean toward black olives, as I do. The small portion of rye flour gives the bread an earthy flavor but by no means turns it into a "rye bread."

INGREDIENTS

1½ cups (355 ml) water, lukewarm

1 tablespoon (15 ml) extra-virgin olive oil

1½ teaspoons kosher salt

1 teaspoon pure maple syrup

1 tablespoon (3 g) dried rosemary

2½ cups (314 g) organic unbleached all-purpose flour

1½ cups (188 g) whole-wheat flour

⅓ cup (32 g) rye flour

1½ teaspoons instant, active dry, or bread machine yeast

1 cup (100 g) chopped olives of your choice

DIRECTIONS

1. Be sure the kneading paddle is attached to the bread pan. Add the water, olive oil, salt, maple syrup, rosemary, flours, and yeast to the bread pan in the order listed.

2. If your bread machine has the French setting, choose that. Otherwise, use the Basic or White setting. Choose the 2-pound (907-g) loaf size. Press start.

3. When the Add-In signal sounds, add the olives.

4. Once the bread has finished baking, remove it from the bread pan. Set it on a wire rack, and let it cool completely before slicing.

Makes one 2-pound (907-g) loaf

Vegan French Baguettes

Your bread machine prepares the baguette dough to perfection with little effort on your part, saving you time while ensuring a consistent texture and flavor. Then you shape the baguettes and finish them in a hot oven. They are perfect for any occasion, whether paired with a hearty soup, used to make sandwiches, or simply enjoyed with a smear of butter.

INGREDIENTS

1 cup plus 2 tablespoons (263 ml) water, lukewarm

1 teaspoon kosher salt

½ teaspoon organic cane sugar

2 tablespoons (14 g) ground flaxseed

1¾ teaspoons instant, active dry, or bread machine yeast

3 cups (360 g) white bread flour

Cornmeal, for dusting the pan

DIRECTIONS

1. Be sure the kneading paddle is attached to your bread machine pan. Add the water, salt, sugar, ground flaxseed, yeast, and flour to the bread pan in the order listed.

2. Select the Dough setting. Press start.

3. Once the cycle has finished, lightly flour a work surface. Punch down on the dough and transfer it to the floured surface. Let it rest, covered with plastic wrap, for 10 minutes.

4. Divide the dough into two equal pieces and shape each into a 12-inch (30-cm)-long baguette.

5. Place them on a baking sheet dusted with cornmeal, loosely cover with plastic wrap, and let rise for 30 to 40 minutes. Meanwhile, preheat your oven to 425°F (220°C) with a pan of hot water on the bottom rack.

6. Dust the risen dough with flour and make four diagonal slashes on each loaf.

7. Bake the baguettes for 25 to 30 minutes until golden brown and hollow sounding when tapped. Cool them on a wire rack before slicing for the best results.

Makes 2 baguettes

Vegan Peppery Parmesan Country French Bread

You'll love the aroma of this bread after it comes out of the machine. Beyond its aromatic allure, this homemade bread serves as a delicious accompaniment to dishes such as lasagna, spaghetti, or an Italian meatball soup.

INGREDIENTS

1¼ cups (295 ml) water, lukewarm

¼ cup (59 ml) extra-virgin olive oil

1½ teaspoons kosher salt

3¾ cups (469 g) organic unbleached all-purpose flour

1 cup (120 g) vegan parmesan cheese (see note)

1 teaspoon coarse black pepper

1½ teaspoons instant, active dry, or bread machine yeast

DIRECTIONS

1. Make sure the kneading paddle is attached to the bread pan. Add the water, olive oil, salt, flour, cheese, pepper, and yeast to the bread pan in the order listed.

2. Choose the French setting if your machine has it. Otherwise, select the Basic or White setting. Choose the desired crust color (if available) and the 2-pound (907-g) loaf size. Press start.

3. Once the bread has finished baking, remove it from the pan. Allow it to completely cool on a wire rack. Slice and serve!

Makes one 2-pound (907-g) loaf

Note: Use grated vegan parmesan if available. If not, buy shredded and pulse it in a blender or food processor to achieve a finer consistency. If you can't find vegan parmesan, use another type of vegan cheese or nutritional yeast. I like Follow Your Heart brand parmesan.

Vegan Bread Machine Buttery Brioche

Just wait until you sink your teeth into this brioche loaf—it's a fluffy, buttery marvel that's so delicious! Perfect for breakfast, brunch, or whenever you need a little slice of heaven that just happens to be plant-based. Enjoy the indulgence!

INGREDIENTS

⅓ cup plus 1½ tablespoons (105 ml) unsweetened almond milk, lukewarm

¼ cup plus 2 tablespoons (83 g) vegan butter, room temperature, cut into ½-inch (1-cm) pieces

¾ cup (173 g) unsweetened plain vegan yogurt

1 teaspoon kosher salt

2 tablespoons (26 g) organic cane sugar

2¾ cups plus 1 tablespoon (352 g) organic unbleached all-purpose flour

2½ teaspoons (10 g) instant, active dry, or bread machine yeast

DIRECTIONS

1. Be sure the kneading paddle is attached to the bread pan. Add the nondairy milk, vegan butter, vegan yogurt, salt, sugar, flour, and yeast to the pan in the order listed.

2. Select the Sweet setting on your bread machine (if available). If not, choose the Basic or White setting. Then choose the 1½-pound (680-g) loaf size. Press start.

3. Once the bread has finished baking, remove it from the bread pan. Set it on a wire rack to cool, then slice and enjoy!

Makes one 1½-pound (680-g) loaf

Vegan Bread Machine Boule

Indulge in the epitome of simplicity and flavor fusion with the Vegan Bread Machine Boule, a culinary masterpiece crafted with love and innovation. From the humble beginnings of cold water, unbleached flour, and instant yeast in the bread machine pan, to the gentle transformation during the dough cycle and the overnight rest that deepens its flavors, this boule promises an irresistible symphony of tastes and textures. With each slice revealing a golden, pillowy interior adorned with artistic slashes, the aroma of freshly baked bread fills the air, igniting a hunger only satisfied by its delicate balance of sweetness and savory notes. With each bite, experience a harmonious blend that dances across the palate, leaving you craving more. This, dear friends, is the Vegan Bread Machine Boule—a testament to the magic of simplicity and the joy of culinary creation.

INGREDIENTS

FOR THE SPONGE

1 cup (235 ml) cold water

1½ cups (188 g) organic unbleached, all-purpose flour

1 teaspoon instant or bread machine yeast

FOR THE DOUGH

3 tablespoons (45 ml) cold water

1 teaspoon sugar

1½ teaspoons salt

2 cups (250 g) organic unbleached, all-purpose flour

¼ teaspoon instant or bread machine yeast

DIRECTIONS

1. To make the sponge: Be sure the kneading paddle is attached to your bread machine pan. Add the cold water, flour, and instant or bread machine yeast to the bread pan in the order listed.

2. Choose the Dough setting and press start. Let it mix for 1 minute. Don't forget to scrape any flour stuck in the corners into the mixing area using a small spatula.

3. Once mixed, unplug the bread machine, close the lid, and let the flour mixture stand at room temperature overnight or for at least 8 hours—but don't exceed 16 hours!

4. To make the dough: Open the lid of the bread machine and add the dough ingredients in the order listed.

5. Press start to restart the dough cycle and monitor after 5 to 10 minutes of mixing. Adjust the dough's consistency by adding additional flour 1 tablespoon (8 g) at a time if too wet, or water if too dry, until you achieve a smooth but slightly tacky ball.

6. Once the dough cycle ends, ensure the dough has doubled in size. If not, allow it to continue rising in the machine until doubled, especially if your kitchen is cool or drafty.

continued >

Vegan Bread Machine Boule

continued

7. To prepare and bake the loaf: Lightly flour a work surface and line a baking sheet with parchment paper. Transfer the dough from the bread machine pan to the floured surface or a silicone baking mat. Shape it into a smooth ball by pulling the dough around to the bottom until the top is smooth, then pinch the bottom.

8. Place the dough ball onto the parchment-covered baking sheet, cover loosely with lightly oiled plastic wrap or a tea towel, and let it rise in a warm place until almost doubled in size.

9. About 15 minutes before baking, preheat a conventional oven to 500°F (260°C). Optionally, sprinkle the top of the loaf with flour and make several cuts across it using a single-edge razor blade or sharp, serrated knife.

10. Reduce the oven temperature to 425°F (220°C) and bake for 30 to 35 minutes, or until the loaf is golden brown and the internal temperature reaches 200°F (93°C).

11. Allow the loaf to cool on a rack before slicing. For neater slices, wait at least an hour before cutting into the bread.

Makes one 2-pound (907-g) loaf

Ciabatta Bread

Utilizing a bread machine is a convenient approach for handling the highly loose and adhesive dough of ciabatta. In this recipe, you'll begin by creating a sponge, a pre-fermentation starter prominent in Italian breadmaking. This technique enhances the flavor and texture of the final loaf by allowing the dough to ferment slowly with a small amount of yeast. The result? Those coveted little airy holes characteristic of ciabatta. I recommend preparing the sponge 12 hours in advance to ensure optimal fermentation and flavor development.

INGREDIENTS

FOR THE OVERNIGHT SPONGE

¾ cup (90 g) white bread flour

½ cup (120 ml) water

Pinch of instant, active dry, or bread machine yeast

FOR THE DOUGH

Proofed overnight sponge

¾ cup (175 ml) water, cool

3 tablespoons (45 ml) extra-virgin olive oil

2½ cups (300 g) white bread flour, plus more for dusting

1½ teaspoons kosher salt

2 teaspoons (8 g) instant, active dry, or bread machine yeast

DIRECTIONS

1. To make the sponge: Place the flour, water, and yeast in a large bowl. Stir it until smooth. Cover it loosely with plastic wrap or a clean, damp tea towel. Let it sit at room temperature for 12 to 24 hours to proof. There should be bubbles and a sour, but pleasant, aroma.

2. When the sponge is ready, be sure the kneading paddle is attached to your bread machine pan. Add the sponge, water, olive oil, flour, salt, and yeast to the bread pan in the order listed.

3. Select the Artisan setting on your bread machine (if available). If not, use the Basic setting. Press start.

4. Once the cycle has finished, line a baking sheet with parchment paper. Transfer the dough to the sheet, and arrange it into an oblong oval shape, about 12 to 14 inches (30 to 36 cm) long.

5. Cover the dough loosely with plastic wrap. Let it rest for 20 minutes.

6. Preheat your oven to 425°F (220°C) with a rack in the middle. Once the oven is ready, remove the plastic wrap from the dough and lightly dust it with some additional flour.

7. Bake on the middle rack for 30 minutes, or until it is lightly brown and sounds hollow when it's tapped.

8. Remove the bread from the oven, and let it cool completely on a wire rack before slicing.

Makes 1 large loaf

Vegan Holy Challah Bread

Delight in the rich and comforting flavors of vegan challah bread, a plant-based adaptation of the classic Jewish favorite. This bread machine–crafted loaf boasts a soft and subtly sweet interior, paired with a golden-brown, egg-free crust—a delightful addition to any occasion.

INGREDIENTS

¾ cup (175 ml) water, lukewarm

¼ cup plus 1 tablespoon (69 g) vegan butter, room temperature, cut into ½-inch (1-cm) pieces

¼ cup (60 ml) aquafaba (page 20)

1 teaspoon kosher salt

3 tablespoons (39 g) organic cane sugar

3 cups (375 g) organic unbleached all-purpose flour

1½ teaspoons instant, active dry, or bread machine yeast

DIRECTIONS

1. Make sure the kneading paddle is attached to the bread machine pan. Add the water, vegan butter, aquafaba, salt, sugar, flour, and yeast to the bread pan in the order listed.

2. If your bread machine has a Sweet setting, choose that; otherwise, select the Basic or White setting. Choose the desired crust color (if available), then choose the 1½-pound (680-g) loaf size. Press start.

3. Once the bread has finished baking, transfer it to a wire rack. Allow it to cool completely before slicing.

Makes one 1½-pound (680-g) loaf

3

FILLED AND FLAVORED BREADS

Simple loaves are wonderful, but sometimes you want something extra special. This chapter celebrates the incredible versatility of the bread machine with stuffed, swirled, and flavor-packed breads. From savory Cajun and vegan cheese bread to aromatic zucchini bread, these recipes take "plain" bread to new heights. With easy step-by-step instructions, you'll master the art of layering ingredients for bakery-quality results every time. Prepare for bread nirvana!

Cajun Bread

Bread machine Cajun bread delivers a fiery kick of spice and savory goodness in every slice. Infused with the bold flavors of Cajun seasoning, this bread has a robust and aromatic profile, with savory notes that linger on the palate.

INGREDIENTS

½ cup (120 ml) water

1 tablespoon (14 g) vegan butter, room temperature, cut into ½-inch (1-cm) pieces

¼ cup (40 g) chopped onions

¼ cup (38 g) chopped green bell peppers

1 tablespoon (13 g) organic cane sugar

2 teaspoons (6 g) finely chopped garlic

2 cups (250 g) white bread flour

1 teaspoon Cajun seasoning

1 teaspoon ground turmeric

1 teaspoon instant, active dry, or bread machine yeast

DIRECTIONS

1. Make sure the kneading paddle is attached to the bread machine pan. Add the water, vegan butter, onions, bell peppers, sugar, garlic, flour, seasoning, turmeric, and yeast to the bread pan in the order listed.

2. Select the Basic or White setting. Do not use the delay cycle. Choose medium crust color (if available), and select the 2-pound (907-g) loaf size. Press start.

3. Once the bread has finished baking, remove it from the bread pan. Transfer it to a wire rack, and let it cool completely before slicing.

Makes one 2-pound (907-g) loaf

Vegan Cheese Bread

Some cheese breads are chunky and heavy. This one has a nice fluffy texture along with the creamy richness. Get ready to melt with delight over vegan bread machine cheese bread! It's like a cheesy hug for your taste buds, minus the dairy drama. With each fluffy slice, you'll wonder how something so deliciously cheesy could be completely plant-powered. So, grab your bread machine and get ready to bake up a storm of dairy-free decadence that even the cows would envy!

INGREDIENTS

1 cup (235 ml) warm water

½ cup (120 ml) melted vegan butter

2 teaspoons (9 g) organic cane sugar

1½ teaspoons kosher salt

2 cups (225 g) shredded vegan cheddar cheese

3 cups (360 g) white bread flour

1½ teaspoons instant, active dry, or bread machine yeast

DIRECTIONS

1. Be sure the kneading paddle is attached to your bread machine pan. Add the water, vegan butter, sugar, salt, cheese, flour, and yeast to the bread pan in the order listed.

2. Choose the Basic or White setting. Select the 2-pound (907-g) loaf size. Press start.

3. Once the bread is finished, remove it from the bread pan. Transfer it to a wire rack to cool before slicing.

Makes one 2-pound (907-g) loaf

Savory Sour Cream and Chive Bread

In this loaf the gentle but assertive kick from the chives is subdued by the subtle tanginess and creaminess of the sour cream. This bread is excellent served warm with a meal, soup, or salad. Or toast it the next day for breakfast.

INGREDIENTS

⅔ cup (160 ml) oat milk, room temperature

¼ cup (60 ml) water, room temperature

¼ cup (60 g) vegan sour cream

2 tablespoons (28 g) vegan butter, room temperature, cut into ½-inch (1-cm) pieces

1½ teaspoons organic cane sugar

1½ teaspoons kosher salt

3 cups (360 g) white bread flour

⅛ teaspoon baking soda

¼ cup (12 g) minced chives

2¼ teaspoons (9 g) instant, active dry, or bread machine yeast

DIRECTIONS

1. Be sure the kneading paddle is fitted in the bread machine pan. Add the oat milk, water, sour cream, vegan butter, sugar, salt, flour, baking soda, chives, and yeast to the bread pan in the order listed.

2. Choose the Basic or White setting. Select the desired crust color (if available), and choose the 2-pound (907-g) loaf size.

3. Once the bread has finished baking, remove it from the pan. Transfer the bread to a wire rack. Let it cool completely before slicing.

Makes one 2-pound (907-g) loaf

Jalapeño Cheddar Bread

The secret to this tantalizing recipe lies in the harmonious dance of shredded vegan cheese, fresh jalapeños, and plant-based butter. It is—a feast of heat and heartiness.

INGREDIENTS

1½ cups (355 ml) vegan buttermilk (see note)

1 teaspoon Frank's RedHot sauce or your favorite hot sauce

3 tablespoons (42 g) vegan butter, room temperature, cut into ½-inch (1-cm) pieces

1 tablespoon (13 g) organic cane sugar

1 teaspoon kosher salt

4 cups (500 g) organic unbleached all-purpose flour

1½ teaspoons instant, active dry, or bread machine yeast

3 tablespoons (23 g) diced jalapeño peppers

1 cup (115 g) shredded vegan cheddar cheese

DIRECTIONS

1. Be sure the kneading paddle is fitted in the bread machine pan. Add the buttermilk, hot sauce, vegan butter, sugar, salt, flour, and yeast to the bread pan in the order listed.

2. Choose the White setting on your bread machine, and choose the desired crust color (if available). Select the loaf size (2-pound [907-g]). Press start.

3. When the Add-In signal sounds, add the jalapeños and vegan cheese so they can be kneaded into the dough.

4. Once the bread has finished baking, remove it from the bread pan. Transfer it to a wire rack. Let it cool completely before slicing.

Makes one 2-pound (907-g) loaf

Note: To make vegan buttermilk: In a bowl, whisk together 1 cup (235 ml) of unsweetened almond milk or soymilk with 1 tablespoon (15 ml) of lemon juice. Let it sit for 5 minutes before using.

Easy Tomato-Basil Bread Machine Bread

Bread machine baking is all about time-saving shortcuts that don't sacrifice flavor. I can't think of a better one than using a good-quality bottled pasta sauce. Serve this alongside a refreshing vegetable pasta salad loaded with a good vegan cheese.

INGREDIENTS

2 cups (456 g) tomato-basil pasta sauce

3 tablespoons (15 g) nutritional yeast or vegan parmesan cheese (see note)

3–4 cups (360–480 g) white bread flour

2¼ teaspoons (9 g) instant, active dry, or bread machine yeast

DIRECTIONS

1. Be sure the kneading paddle is attached to your bread machine pan. Combine the pasta sauce, nutritional yeast or vegan cheese, 3 cups (360 g) of the bread flour, and yeast in the bread pan. Choose the Basic or White. Select the 2-pound (907-g) loaf size setting and press start.

2. With the machine lid open, slowly incorporate additional bread flour, 1 tablespoon (8 g) at a time, until the mixture transforms into a smooth, soft ball.

3. Close the lid. Once the bread has finished baking, promptly take the bread out of the machine. Let it cool on a wire rack before slicing.

Makes one 2-pound (907-g) loaf

Note: Use grated vegan parmesan if available. If not, buy shredded and pulse it in a blender or food processor to achieve a finer consistency. I like Follow Your Heart brand parmesan.

Savory Bread Machine Onion Bread

This is the bread I make when I want the kitchen to smell incredibly good as the bread bakes. When they are in season, I always use Vidalias, Maui Mauis, or other sweet onions in this recipe.

INGREDIENTS

1 cup (235 ml) water

1⅛ teaspoons kosher salt

1 tablespoon (13 g) organic cane sugar

2 tablespoons (28 g) vegan butter, room temperature, cut into ½-inch (1-cm) pieces

3 tablespoons (36 g) minced yellow or sweet onions

3½ cups (420 g) white bread flour

2 teaspoons (8 g) instant, active dry, or bread machine yeast

DIRECTIONS

1. Be sure the kneading paddle is attached to your bread machine pan. Add the water, salt, sugar, vegan butter, onions, flour, and yeast to the bread pan in the order listed.

2. Select the Basic or White setting. Select the 1½-pound (680-g) loaf size, and choose medium for the crust color (if available). Press start.

3. Once the bread is finished, remove it from the pan and gently remove the kneading paddle.

4. Let the bread cool for 10 to 15 minutes before slicing.

Makes one 1½-pound (680-g) loaf

Kalamata Olive Bread

The bold, briny flavor of premium kalamata olives is one of my favorite vegan bread ingredients. You can make a milder olive bread if you use ¼ cup (60 g) of olives or a more assertive loaf using ¾ cup (90 g); the rest of the recipe remains the same.

INGREDIENTS

½ cup (120 ml) kalamata olive brine (juice from 1 or 2 jars of olives)

1 cup (235 ml) warm water

2 tablespoons (30 ml) extra-virgin olive oil

3 cups (360 g) white bread flour

1⅔ cups (208 g) whole-wheat flour

1½ teaspoons kosher salt

2 tablespoons (26 g) organic cane sugar

2 teaspoons (3 g) dried basil

2 teaspoons (8 g) instant, active dry, or bread machine yeast

½ cup (50 g) finely chopped kalamata olives

DIRECTIONS

1. Be sure the kneading paddle is attached to your bread machine pan. Combine the olive brine and warm water in a large measuring cup.

2. Add the olive oil, flours, salt, sugar, basil, and yeast to the bread pan in the order listed.

3. Select the Wheat or Basic setting. Choose the desired crust color (if available) and the 2-pound (907-g) loaf size.

4. Add the olives when the Add-In signal sounds.

5. Once the olive bread has finished baking, remove it from the bread machine and allow it to cool for 15 to 20 minutes before slicing.

Makes one 2-pound (907-g) loaf

Vegan Parmesan Garlic Bread

This parmesan garlic bread is moist and flavorful, and it is great without any butter. But, for an extra touch of indulgence, try it with a luscious spread of vegan butter on each slice.

INGREDIENTS

1⅓ cups (315 ml) water

⅓ cup (79 ml) extra-virgin olive oil

¼ cup (55 g) vegan butter, melted

1 tablespoon (10 g) minced garlic

3½ cups (439 g) organic unbleached all-purpose flour

½ cup (60 g) vegan parmesan cheese (see note)

1 teaspoon garlic powder

2 teaspoons (3 g) dried basil

2 teaspoons (2 g) dried oregano

2 teaspoons (10 g) kosher salt

3 tablespoons (39 g) organic cane sugar

2¼ teaspoons (9 g) instant, active dry, or bread machine yeast

DIRECTIONS

1. Be sure the kneading paddle is attached to your bread machine pan. Add the water, olive oil, butter, minced garlic, flour, vegan parmesan, garlic powder, basil, oregano, salt, sugar, and yeast to the bread pan in the order listed.

2. Choose the Basic setting. Choose the light crust color or your preferred crust option (if available), and select the 2-pound (907-g) loaf size. Press start.

3. After the bread is done, transfer it to a wire rack. Let it cool for 10 minutes before slicing.

Makes one 2-pound (907-g) loaf

Note: Use grated vegan parmesan if available. If not, buy shredded and pulse it in a blender or food processor to achieve a finer consistency. I like Follow Your Heart brand parmesan.

Cranberry Pecan Rosemary Bread

This flavorful bread combines dried cranberries and toasted pecans, enhancing the freshness of rosemary. The result is a delightful, whole-wheat artisan loaf with a beautiful brown crust. Simply mix and knead the dough in a bread machine, followed by baking in a conventional oven.

INGREDIENTS

FOR THE STARTER

1 cup (235 ml) water

1½ cups (188 g) whole-wheat flour

1 teaspoon instant, active dry, or bread machine yeast

FOR THE DOUGH

⅓ cup (80 ml) water, plus more if needed

1 tablespoon (20 g) pure maple syrup

1½ teaspoons kosher salt

1¾ cups (210 g) white bread flour, plus more if needed

¼ teaspoon instant, active dry, or bread machine yeast

1 tablespoon (3 g) dried rosemary

½ cup (55 g) chopped pecans, toasted

¾ cup (80 g) dried cranberries

FOR THE GLAZE

1 tablespoon (15 ml) almond milk

1 tablespoon (20 g) pure maple syrup

DIRECTIONS

1. To make the starter: Be sure the kneading paddle is attached to your bread machine pan. Add the water, flour, and yeast to the bread pan in the order listed.

2. Choose the Dough setting. Press start. Let the machine blend for about 5 minutes. Use a small spatula to carefully nudge any flour stuck in the corners into the mixing area.

3. Unplug the machine. Allow the starter to rest in the bread machine pan at room temperature overnight or for about 8 hours.

4. To make the dough: Add the water, maple syrup, salt, bread flour, and yeast to the starter in the bread machine pan.

5. Select the Dough setting. Press start.

6. Monitor the dough at least twice by lifting the lid. Initially, check right after the machine begins mixing to ensure proper paddle engagement. The dough should begin to clump. Adjust the consistency by adding water or flour as needed. If it's too dry, add 1 tablespoon of water (15 ml) or 1 tablespoon (8 g) of flour if it's too wet.

7. After 15 minutes into the cycle, check the dough's consistency. It should stick to the side and then pull away cleanly.

8. When the Add-In signal sounds, add the rosemary, pecans, and dried cranberries.

9. Once the cycle concludes, check the dough. If necessary, allow more time for rising, especially if your kitchen is cold. Leave the dough in the machine until it doubles in size.

continued >

Cranberry Pecan Rosemary Bread

continued

10. To prepare and bake the loaf: Lightly flour a work surface, and line a baking sheet with parchment paper. Transfer the dough to the floured surface, and briefly knead it to remove bubbles.

11. Roll the dough into an 8- × 12-inch (20- × 30-cm) oblong shape. Roll it up from the long side, pinch the seam, and turn the ends under to seal. Shape the dough into a rounded oval.

12. Place the dough on the baking sheet. Cover it loosely with a clean dish towel. Let it rise in a warm place until almost double in size. About 15 minutes before baking, preheat your oven to 425°F (220°C).

13. To glaze the dough: Use a single-edge razor blade or a sharp, serrated knife to make several cuts across the top of the bread about ½ inch (1 cm) deep. Mix the almond milk and maple syrup in a small bowl. Brush on the glaze with a basting brush.

14. Bake for 25 to 30 minutes until the loaf is golden brown and the internal temperature reaches 200°F (93°C).

15. Allow the loaf to cool on a wire rack before slicing.

Makes 1 large loaf

Peanut Butter Bread

What better way to enjoy a PB & J than on actual peanut butter bread? This bread is perfect for a "sweet sandwich." Can't wait for lunch? Have it for breakfast with your morning coffee. Hungry before dinner? This makes a delicious afternoon snack.

INGREDIENTS

1⅛ cups (263 ml) water, lukewarm

¼ cup (65 g) natural creamy peanut butter

3 cups (360 g) white bread flour

3 tablespoons (45 g) packed light brown sugar

½ teaspoon kosher salt

2 teaspoons (8 g) instant, active dry, or bread machine yeast

DIRECTIONS

1. Be sure the kneading paddle is attached to your bread machine pan. Add the water, peanut butter, flour, brown sugar, salt, and yeast to the bread pan in the order listed.

2. Select the Sweet setting, and choose the light crust color (if available) and the 2-pound (907-g) loaf size. Press start.

3. Once the bread is finished, remove it from the bread pan. Transfer it to a wire rack, and let it cool completely before slicing.

Makes one 2-pound (907-g) loaf

Garlic Pull-Apart Bubble Loaf

Pull-apart bubble loaves are fun to snack on: You just tear off the exact-size piece you would like. They are also fun for dipping in sauces and gravies.

INGREDIENTS

FOR THE BREAD

½ cup (120 ml) water, lukewarm, plus more if needed

½ cup (115 g) vegan sour cream

2 tablespoons (28 g) vegan butter, room temperature, cut into ½-inch (1-cm) pieces

3 tablespoons (39 g) organic cane sugar

1½ teaspoons kosher salt

3 cups (360 g) white bread flour, plus more if needed

2¼ teaspoons (9 g) instant, active dry, or bread machine yeast

FOR THE GARLIC-HERB BUTTER

¼ cup (55 g) vegan butter, melted

1½ tablespoons (15 g) minced garlic

1 teaspoon Italian seasoning

DIRECTIONS

1. Be sure the kneading paddle is attached to your bread machine pan. Add the water, vegan sour cream, vegan butter, sugar, salt, flour, and yeast to the bread pan in the order listed.

2. Select the Dough setting. Press start, and check the dough after 5 minutes of mixing. If necessary, add 1 to 2 tablespoons of water or flour.

3. Once the cycle is complete, lightly flour a work surface. Transfer the dough to the floured surface, cover it with a tea towel, and let it rest for 15 minutes.

4. Divide the dough into 36 pieces, and shape each into a ball.

5. To make the garlic-herb butter: Combine the melted butter, garlic, and Italian seasoning in a shallow bowl. Dip each dough ball into the mixture and place them in a non-greased 9- × 5-inch (23- × 12-cm) loaf pan.

6. Cover it with a tea towel and allow the dough to rise in a warm place until doubled, about 45 minutes. When the rising time is nearly complete, preheat your oven to 375°F (190°C).

7. Bake for 35 to 40 minutes, or until the bread is golden brown. If the bread browns too quickly, loosely cover it with foil.

8. When the baking has finished, remove the bread from the pan and place it on a wire rack. Serve the bread warm.

Makes 36 golf ball–size pieces

Vegan Zucchini Bread

Zucchini bread made in a bread machine is a delightful treat that combines the moist texture of shredded zucchini, and aromatic spices such as cinnamon and nutmeg, with the warm, comforting flavor of freshly baked bread.

INGREDIENTS

⅓ cup (79 ml) vegetable oil

¾ cup (90 g) shredded zucchini

2 small overripe bananas

⅓ cup (75 g) packed light brown sugar

3 tablespoons (39 g) organic cane sugar

1½ cups (188 g) organic unbleached all-purpose flour

½ teaspoon kosher salt

1 teaspoon pumpkin pie spice

½ teaspoon baking soda

½ teaspoon baking powder

⅓ cup (40 g) chopped walnuts

DIRECTIONS

1. Be sure the kneading paddle is attached to your bread machine pan. Lightly spray the inside of the bread pan with cooking spray or lightly brush with vegetable oil.

2. Add the oil, zucchini, bananas, brown sugar, cane sugar, flour, salt, pumpkin pie spice, baking soda, baking powder, and walnuts to the bread pan in the order listed.

3. Select the Cake setting and the 2-pound (907-g) loaf size. Press start.

4. Scrape down the sides with a rubber spatula while the batter is mixing. This will ensure all the ingredients are fully incorporated. Once they are incorporated, you can stop and allow the machine to continue.

5. Once the cycle has finished, remove the bread from the machine. Transfer it to a wire rack, and allow the zucchini bread to cool before slicing.

Makes one 2-pound (907-g) loaf

CHAPTER

4

GLUTEN-FREE VEGAN BREADS

For those who avoid gluten, the bread machine opens a whole new world of fresh-baked possibilities. This chapter explores gluten-free flours and recipes to craft incredibly light and flavorful loaves right in your own kitchen. From tender sandwich breads to gluten-free pizza dough, you'll be amazed at the airy, never-dense texture achievable with a few simple ingredients and your trusty bread maker. Enjoy all the comforts of homemade bread once again!

Gluten-Free Sandwich Bread

Think you can't have a decent everyday sandwich bread that's both vegan and gluten-free? Well, prepare to have your mind blown faster than a gluten-free bagel in a toaster! This bread is the unicorn of the bakery aisle—vegan, gluten-free, and deliciously sandwich-worthy. So, bid farewell to those sad, crumbly loaves of yesteryear and say hello to a gluten-free revolution that's as tasty as it is revolutionary!

INGREDIENTS

1 cup (235 ml) water, lukewarm

¼ cup (55 g) vegan butter, room temperature, cut into ½-inch (1-cm) pieces

¾ cup (175 ml) aquafaba (see page 20)

1½ teaspoons kosher salt

3 tablespoons (39 g) organic cane sugar

3¼ cups (442 g) gluten-free all-purpose baking flour (I like Bob's Red Mill; see note.)

3 tablespoons (21 g) ground flaxseed

2 teaspoons (8 g) instant, active dry, or bread machine yeast

DIRECTIONS

1. Attach the kneading paddle to the bread machine pan. Add the water, vegan butter, aquafaba, salt, sugar, flour, ground flaxseed, and yeast to the bread pan in the order listed.

2. Choose the Gluten-Free setting on your bread machine. Then select the 1½-pound (680-g) loaf size. Press start.

3. Once the bread is finished, remove it from the bread pan. Place it on a wire rack to cool, then slice and enjoy!

Makes one 1½-pound (680-g) loaf

Note: Be sure to use a gluten-free all-purpose baking flour or bread flour. A regular 1:1 flour will not yield good results. Be sure to read the labels as they will specify.

Gluten-Free Cinnamon Swirl Bread

Gluten-free-bread bakers have experimented with a lot of non-wheat flours, such as almond flour, over the years. But I have never found a one-grain flour that is perfect for the bread machine. Blends such as Bob's Red Mill Gluten-free 1:1 Baking Flour always work best.

INGREDIENTS

FOR THE DOUGH

1 cup (235 ml) water, lukewarm

¼ cup (55 g) vegan butter, room temperature, cut into ½-inch (1-cm) pieces

¾ cup (173 g) unsweetened plain vegan yogurt

1½ teaspoons kosher salt

¼ cup (50 g) organic cane sugar

3¼ cups (481 g) 1:1 gluten-free flour blend (Bob's Red Mill Gluten-free 1:1 Baking Flour is my favorite.)

3 tablespoons (21 g) ground flaxseed

2 teaspoons (8 g) instant, active dry, or bread machine yeast

FOR THE CINNAMON SWIRL

¼ cup (50 g) organic cane sugar

2 teaspoons (5 g) ground cinnamon

DIRECTIONS

1. Attach the kneading paddle to the bread machine pan. Add the water, vegan butter, vegan yogurt, salt, sugar, flour blend, ground flaxseed, and yeast to the bread pan in the order listed.

2. Select the Gluten-Free setting on your bread machine. Then choose the 1½-pound (680-g) loaf size. Press start.

3. While the bread is being prepared, make the cinnamon swirl: Add the sugar and cinnamon to a small bowl. Whisk thoroughly to combine, and set it aside.

4. Once the paddle signal goes off, pause the bread machine. Remove the dough and the kneading paddle. Heavily dust a clean surface with the gluten-free flour.

5. Place the dough on the floured surface. Roll it away from you until it is a rectangle about 14 to 16 inches (36 to 41 cm) long and ¼ inch (6 mm) thick.

6. Evenly cover the surface of the dough with the cinnamon swirl mixture. Roll the dough lengthwise into a tight log shape and fold and seal the ends tightly.

7. Place the dough into the bread pan (without the kneading paddle), and press start.

8. When the bread has finished baking, remove it from the bread pan. Let it completely cool on a wire rack. Then slice it and enjoy!

Makes one 1½-pound (680-g) loaf

Hearty Multigrain Gluten-Free Bread

Versatile, nutritious, and delicious, this gluten-free hearty multigrain bread machine bread is your ticket to gluten-free glory! Say goodbye to those cardboard-like gluten-free loaves that crumble at the mere sight of a butter knife. With a texture so satisfying, you'll wonder why you ever bothered with gluten in the first place. So go ahead, slather on that avocado or stack it high with your favorite fixings—this bread can handle it all with gluten-free finesse!

INGREDIENTS

1 cup (235 ml) water, lukewarm

¼ cup (55 g) vegan butter, room temperature, cut into ½-inch (1-cm) pieces

¾ cup (175 ml) aquafaba (see page 20)

2 cups (272 g) gluten-free all-purpose baking flour (I like Bob's Red Mill.)

1 cup (120 g) oat flour

¼ cup plus 2 tablespoons (39 g) ground flaxseed

2 teaspoons (8 g) instant, active dry, or bread machine yeast

DIRECTIONS

1. Be sure the kneading paddle is attached to your bread machine pan. Add the water, vegan butter, aquafaba, flours, ground flaxseed, and yeast to the bread pan in the order listed.

2. Select the 1½-pound (680-g) loaf size. Press start.

3. Once the bread is finished, remove it from the bread pan. Transfer it to a wire rack to cool completely before slicing.

Makes one 1½-pound (680-g) loaf

Gluten-Free Bread Machine Pizza Dough

Making gluten-free pizza dough in a bread machine is super easy. Simply combine the ingredients and let the machine do the work through the dough cycle. Once the dough is ready, shape it into pizza crusts, add your toppings, and bake it for a delicious gluten-free pizza experience.

INGREDIENTS

1¼ cups (295 ml) water, lukewarm

¼ cup (59 ml) extra-virgin olive oil

1 teaspoon apple cider vinegar

3½ teaspoons (14 g) instant, active dry, or bread machine yeast

3½ cups (476 g) gluten-free all-purpose baking flour (I like Bob's Red Mill.)

2 tablespoons (26 g) organic cane sugar

1 tablespoon (9 g) xanthan gum (See page 20; omit if your flour blend has it already.)

1½ teaspoons kosher salt

DIRECTIONS

1. Be sure the kneading paddle is attached to the bread machine pan. Add the water, olive oil, apple cider vinegar, yeast, flour, sugar, xanthan gum (if using), and salt to the bread pan in the order listed.

2. Turn on the Dough cycle. Stop the machine before the dough starts rising.

3. Preheat your oven to 400°F (200°C).

4. Place parchment paper on pizza pans, leaving about 1 to 2 inches (2.5 to 5 cm) around the edges. You can also use a cookie sheet and shape it into a round. Divide the dough in half. Use a spatula sprayed with nonstick spray, or oil your hands to shape it into circles.

5. Bake the crusts for 10 to 12 minutes. Add sauce and toppings, then bake for another 12 to 15 minutes until bubbly and golden on the edges.

Makes dough for two 12-inch (30-cm) round pizzas

5

ROLLS, BUNS, AND SPECIALTY BREADS

While loaves are wonderful, sometimes you want something a bit more fun and indulgent. This chapter celebrates the incredible versatility of the bread machine for all sorts of rolls, buns, and unique specialty breads. From decadent orange rolls for breakfast to easy cinnamon rolls and chewy soft pretzels, you'll be amazed at what you can create. These recipes add an extra touch of homemade joy to any meal or occasion. Get ready to impress!

Sweet and Buttery Vegan Bread Machine Cornbread

Most recipes in this book are easier in the bread machine than by traditional methods. But I admit that it's not hard to whip up a batch of cornbread without using a bread machine. Still, I like the consistent texture and flavor you get in a machine-made loaf and the loaf shape itself.

INGREDIENTS

1¼ cups (295 ml) unsweetened almond milk, lukewarm

¼ cup plus 2 tablespoons (83 g) vegan butter, room temperature, cut into ½-inch (1-cm) pieces

½ cup (120 ml) aquafaba (see page 20)

1½ cups (188 g) organic unbleached all-purpose flour

1 cup (140 g) yellow cornmeal

1 cup (200 g) organic cane sugar

1 teaspoon baking powder

1 teaspoon baking soda

½ teaspoon kosher salt

DIRECTIONS

1. Make sure the kneading paddle is attached to the bread machine pan. Add the nondairy milk, vegan butter, aquafaba, flour, cornmeal, sugar, baking powder, baking soda, and salt to the bread pan in the order listed.

2. Select the Cake setting. Choose the light crust color (if available) and the 2-pound (907-g) loaf size. Press start.

3. Once the bread has finished, transfer it to a wire rack. Let it cool for 5 to 10 minutes before slicing.

Makes one 2-pound (907-g) loaf

Bread Machine Vegan Orange Rolls

This straightforward recipe for vegan orange rolls with a bread machine makes the process easy. You begin by crafting a foolproof dough in your bread maker, then roll it out and bake it in your oven for delightful, golden-brown breakfast rolls. They have a mildly sweet taste with a vibrant burst of orange flavor. Serve these delicately drizzled with glaze or double the glaze recipe for complete coverage.

INGREDIENTS

FOR THE DOUGH

1¼ cups (295 ml) oat milk

1 teaspoon pure vanilla extract

½ teaspoon orange extract

3 tablespoons (42 g) vegan butter, room temperature, cut into ½-inch (1-cm) pieces

3 cups (375 g) organic unbleached all-purpose flour

3 tablespoons (39 g) organic cane sugar

1½ teaspoons kosher salt

2 teaspoons (8 g) instant, active dry, or bread machine yeast

FOR THE FILLING

1 tablespoon (14 g) vegan butter, softened for the baking pan

5 tablespoons (69 g) vegan butter

⅓ cup (66 g) organic cane sugar

FOR THE ORANGE GLAZE

1 cup (120 g) confectioners' sugar, plus more if needed

2 tablespoons (28 ml) orange juice, plus more if needed

Notes: You can prepare the rolls a day ahead by assembling them and refrigerating them before the initial rise in the baking pan. Cover the rolls with plastic wrap and allow them to rise for 1 hour on the counter before baking the next day.

For freezing, assemble the rolls and freeze them in the baking pan before the rise. Place the frozen rolls in the fridge overnight, and then let them thaw for 1 hour on the counter before baking.

DIRECTIONS

1. Be sure the kneading paddle is attached to your bread machine pan. Add the nondairy milk, vanilla, orange extract, and vegan butter to the bread pan in the order listed.

2. Spoon the flour on top of the wet ingredients, sprinkle the sugar and salt around the pan, then create a well in the flour center for the yeast. Place the pan in the bread machine. Select the Dough setting. Press start.

3. Once the dough is ready, coat a 9- × 13-inch (23- × 33-cm) baking pan with the tablespoon (14 g) of softened butter.

4. Lightly flour a work surface. Transfer the dough to the floured surface, and roll it into a 20- × 12-inch (51- × 30-cm) rectangle. Melt the 5 tablespoons (69 g) of vegan butter, then spread it evenly on the rolled dough with a pastry brush. Sprinkle the sugar over the dough, and roll it into a log. Cut it into 12 slices, and arrange them in the prepared pan.

5. Cover the pan with plastic wrap, and let the orange rolls rise in a warm place for 20 to 30 minutes until doubled in size. Close to the end of the rising time, preheat your oven to 375°F (190°C).

6. Remove the plastic wrap and bake the rolls for 20 to 25 minutes, or until golden brown.

7. To make the glaze: Whisk the confectioners' sugar and orange juice until smooth. Adjust the thickness by adding more juice or sugar.

8. Drizzle the warm orange rolls with the glaze.

Makes 12 small rolls

Bread Machine Vegan Hamburger Buns

If you're in search of the perfect vegan hamburger bun, light and fluffy, your quest ends here. Whether adorned with sesame seeds or left plain, their comforting visual appeal is undeniable.

INGREDIENTS

¼ cup (60 ml) aquafaba (see page 20)

½ cup (120 ml) vegan milk

¼ cup (60 ml) water

2 tablespoons (28 g) vegan butter, room temperature, cut into ½-inch (1-cm) pieces

1 tablespoon (13 g) organic cane sugar

¾ teaspoon kosher salt

2½ cups (314 g) organic unbleached all-purpose flour

1⅛ teaspoons instant, active dry, or bread machine yeast

DIRECTIONS

1. Be sure the kneading paddle is attached to your bread machine pan. Add the aquafaba, nondairy milk, water, vegan butter, sugar, salt, flour, and yeast to the bread pan in the order listed.

2. Select the Dough setting. Press start.

3. When the cycle has finished, lightly flour a work surface and line a baking sheet with parchment paper.

4. Transfer the dough to the floured surface. Cut the dough into six or eight equal pieces. Form each piece into a ball, and place it on the prepared baking sheet. Cover your fingertips with flour and flatten each dough ball until it is about ½ inch (1 cm) thick.

5. Cover the baking sheet with a clean tea towel. Set it in a warm place, and let the dough rise until doubled in size, about 30 to 35 minutes. Close to the end of rising time, preheat your oven to 400°F (200°C).

6. Bake the buns for 10 to 12 minutes, or until golden brown.

7. Remove the buns from the oven, and transfer them to a wire rack to cool.

Makes 6 to 8 buns

Fluffy Potato Rolls

These extra-big bread machine potato rolls are irresistibly soft and fluffy. In fact, serious bread bakers have for years added potato, in one form or another, to give breads a softer texture.

INGREDIENTS

½ cup (120 ml) unsweetened soymilk

¼ cup (60 ml) warm water

½ cup (115 g) mashed potatoes

¼ cup (55 g) vegan butter, room temperature, cut into ½-inch (1-cm) pieces

3 tablespoons (45 ml) aquafaba (see page 20)

¼ cup (50 g) organic cane sugar

1½ teaspoons kosher salt

3 cups (360 g) white bread flour

2 teaspoons (8 g) instant, active dry, or bread machine yeast

FOR THE GLAZE

1 tablespoon (20 g) pure maple syrup

1 tablespoon (15 ml) nondairy milk

DIRECTIONS

1. Be sure the kneading paddle is attached to your bread machine pan. Add the nondairy milk, water, mashed potatoes, vegan butter, aquafaba, sugar, salt, flour, and yeast to the bread pan in the order listed.

2. Select the Dough setting. Press start.

3. When the cycle is finished, lightly flour a work surface and grease a round 9-inch (23-cm) pan.

4. Remove the dough from the machine to the floured surface. Divide the dough into 12 equal portions and form them into smooth balls. Evenly arrange the balls in the prepared pan.

5. Cover with a clean tea towel and let rise in a warm, draft-free place until doubled in size, usually about 45 minutes. Close to the end of rising time, preheat your oven to 350°F (175°C).

6. Make the glaze: Combine the maple syrup and nondairy milk in a small bowl. Whisk until smooth.

7. Brush each roll with the glaze. Bake the rolls for 25 to 30 minutes, or until golden.

8. Remove the rolls from the pan, and let them cool on a wire rack.

Makes 12 large rolls

Sweet Potato Rolls

These golden-brown sweet potato rolls are incredible. They have a buttery crust and just the right touch of sweetness. They are excellent alongside robust soups, fresh salads, and hearty stews. They're also handy for sopping up flavorful sauces or simply for eating as a snack with a spread of butter.

INGREDIENTS

1 cup (230 g) mashed sweet potatoes

¾ cup (175 ml) unsweetened almond milk

3 tablespoons (42 g) vegan butter, melted, plus more for brushing the rolls

3 tablespoons (45 ml) aquafaba (see page 20)

4 cups (500 g) organic unbleached all-purpose flour

¼ cup (50 g) organic cane sugar

1 teaspoon kosher salt

2¼ teaspoons (9 g) instant, active dry, or bread machine yeast

DIRECTIONS

1. Be sure the kneading paddle is attached to your bread machine pan. Add the sweet potatoes, nondairy milk, vegan butter, aquafaba, flour, sugar, salt, and yeast to the bread pan in the order listed.

2. Select the Dough setting. Press start.

3. Once the cycle finishes, evenly divide the dough into 16 to 18 pieces. Shape them into balls.

4. Grease a 9-inch (23-cm) baking pan. Place the dough balls in it so they're just touching but not too close.

5. Place the pan in a warm, draft-free place and cover the rolls with a clean tea towel. Let the rolls rise for about 45 minutes. Close to the end of rising time, preheat your oven to 375°F (190°C).

6. Bake the rolls for 20 to 23 minutes, until they brown nicely. Brush the tops with some melted vegan butter and enjoy.

Makes 16 to 18 rolls

Bread Machine Hot Cross Buns

Enlist your bread machine and make cooking an Easter feast a lot easier, especially if there are vegans among your guests.

INGREDIENTS

FOR THE BUNS

1 cup (235 ml) unsweetened almond milk, room temperature

Bob's Red Mill vegan egg replacer for 1 egg

¼ cup (60 g) lightly packed brown sugar

¼ cup (55 g) vegan butter, room temperature, cut into ½-inch (1-cm) pieces

1 teaspoon pure vanilla extract

3½ cups (439 g) organic unbleached all-purpose flour

1 teaspoon ground cinnamon

½ teaspoon allspice

1¼ teaspoons kosher salt

1¼ teaspoons instant, active dry, or bread machine yeast

½ cup (75 g) raisins

FOR THE GLAZE

4½ teaspoons (12 g) confectioners' sugar

1 tablespoon (15 ml) warm water

FOR THE ICING

½ cup (60 g) confectioners' sugar

1 tablespoon (15 ml) nondairy milk of your choice

¼ teaspoon pure vanilla extract

DIRECTIONS

1. Be sure the kneading paddle is attached to your bread machine pan. Add the nondairy milk, egg replacer, brown sugar, vegan butter, vanilla, flour, cinnamon, allspice, salt, and yeast to the bread pan in the order listed.

2. Select the Dough setting. Press start.

3. Add the raisins when the Add-In signal sounds.

4. Once the cycle is finished, lightly flour a work surface. Transfer the dough to the floured surface. Cover it with a clean tea towel. Allow it to rise for 15 minutes.

5. After the rise, divide the dough into 12 portions.

6. Grease an 8- × 8-inch (20- × 20-cm) baking pan with butter or line it with parchment paper. Lightly flour your hands, and shape the dough into buns: Form each portion into a ball, keeping the tops taut by tucking the dough underneath as you roll.

7. Place the buns in the baking pan, evenly spaced, in three rows of four. Cover with a clean tea towel.

8. Let the buns rest and rise in a warm place for 1 hour, or until the dough doubles in size. Close to the end of rising time, preheat your oven to 350°F (175°C).

9. Bake the buns for 25 minutes , or until the tops are golden brown and sound hollow when tapped.

10. Immediately after removing the buns from the oven, prepare the glaze: Stir the confectioners' sugar and warm water together in a small bowl. Brush the glaze on the bun tops.

11. Allow the buns to rest in the pan for about 20 minutes, then transfer them to a plate. While the buns cool, make the icing: Add the confectioners' sugar, nondairy milk, and vanilla to a small bowl. Stir until smooth.

12. Once the buns are completely cooled, pipe crosses on them: Place the icing in a small ziptop bag. Cut a small corner of the bag, then pipe the icing onto the buns. Enjoy!

Makes 12 buns

Easy-to-Make Cinnamon Rolls

Elevate your breakfast routine with homemade cinnamon rolls made almost effortlessly in a bread machine. Just toss the ingredients into the machine, and let it work its magic on the dough. Then roll, fill, and bake. Enjoy warm, gooey cinnamon perfection without the fuss of traditional baking. Watch people's faces when they find out the rolls are vegan . . . a total "shock to the system"!

INGREDIENTS

2½ tablespoons (38 ml) warm water plus 1 tablespoon (7 g) ground flaxseed, for the flax egg

2 teaspoons (8 g) instant, active dry, or bread machine yeast

3⅓ cups (417 g) organic unbleached all-purpose flour

3 tablespoons (39 g) organic cane sugar

¾ teaspoon kosher salt

¼ cup (55 g) vegan butter

1 cup (235 ml) almond milk

3 tablespoons (45 ml) water

FOR THE FILLING

¾ cup (170 g) packed brown sugar

3¾ teaspoons (6 g) ground cinnamon

2 tablespoons (28 g) vegan butter, softened

FOR THE GLAZE

¾ cup (90 g) confectioners' sugar

¼ teaspoon pure vanilla extract

2–3 teaspoons (10–15 ml) almond milk

continued >

Easy-to-Make Cinnamon Rolls

continued

DIRECTIONS

1. Be sure the kneading paddle is attached to your bread machine pan. In a small bowl, stir together the warm water and ground flaxseed until well combined. Let it sit for 10 minutes. Makes 1 flax egg.

2. Begin by placing the yeast, flour, sugar, and salt in the bread pan in the order listed.

3. Melt the butter in the microwave. Mix it with the flax egg, nondairy milk, and water in a small bowl. Pour this mixture onto the dry ingredients in the bread pan. Select the Dough setting. Press start.

4. Once the dough is ready, lightly flour a work surface. Transfer the dough to the floured surface and knead in enough flour for easy handling.

5. Allow the dough to rest for 10 minutes. Grease a 9- × 13-inch (23- × 33-cm) baking pan. Then, make the filling: Combine the brown sugar, cinnamon, and softened butter in a small bowl.

6. Roll out the dough into a ¼-inch (6-mm)-thick rectangular shape on the floured surface.

7. Spread the filling over the entire surface of the dough using a spoon, then roll it up. Cut the rolled dough into 10 to 12 1-inch (2.5-cm)-thick circles and place them in the greased pan.

8. Cover the rolls with a clean tea towel. Let them rise in a warm place for about 30 minutes, until doubled in size.

9. Bake the rolls in a 350°F (175°C) oven for about 25 minutes, or until they turn light brown on top.

10. Close to the end of baking time, make the glaze: Combine the confectioners' sugar, vanilla, and nondairy milk in a small bowl. Start with 2 teaspoons (10 ml) of milk. Stir until smooth, adding the remaining teaspoon if needed. Set it aside.

11. When the rolls are finished baking, swirl the glaze over the baked buns and serve.

Makes 10 to 12 cinnamon rolls

Bread Machine Breadsticks

When I buy breadsticks at the supermarket I often find them to taste slightly stale, nothing like the fresh ones you get in a good restaurant. So, I set out to make better ones in the bread machine, and I am very happy with the results. I hope you like them too.

INGREDIENTS

1 cup (235 ml) water, lukewarm, plus more if needed

3 tablespoons (42 g) vegan butter, softened

1½ teaspoons kosher salt

3 cups (360 g) white bread flour, plus more if needed

2 tablespoons (26 g) organic cane sugar

1 teaspoon Italian seasoning

1 teaspoon garlic powder

2¼ teaspoons (9 g) instant, active dry, or bread machine yeast

2 tablespoons (28 g) vegan butter, melted, for brushing

Vegan parmesan (see note) or nutritional yeast, for serving (optional)

DIRECTIONS

1. Attach the kneading paddle to the bread machine pan. Add the water, vegan butter, salt, flour, sugar, Italian seasoning, garlic powder, and yeast to the bread pan in the order listed.

2. Select the Dough setting. Press start. Inspect the dough after 5 minutes of mixing; adjust with 1 to 2 tablespoons (15 to 30 ml) of water or flour if necessary.

3. Once the cycle concludes, lightly flour a work surface and grease two baking sheets.

4. Transfer the dough to the floured surface and divide it in half. Cut each portion into 12 pieces; shape each into a 4- to 6-inch (10- to 15-cm) rope. Position them 2 inches (5 cm) apart on the baking sheets.

5. Cover with a tea towel and allow the breadsticks to rise in a warm place until doubled, about 20 minutes. Close to the end of rising time, preheat your oven to 350°F (175°C).

6. Bake the breadsticks for 15 to 18 minutes, or until they achieve a golden-brown hue.

7. Take the breadsticks out of the oven. Promptly brush them with melted vegan butter. Sprinkle them with vegan parmesan or nutritional yeast, if desired.

Makes 2 dozen breadsticks

> **Note:** Use grated vegan parmesan if available. If not, buy shredded and pulse it in a blender or food processor to achieve a finer consistency. I like Follow Your Heart brand parmesan.

Vegan Buttery Garlic-Herb Knots

Cheesy goodness meets plant-based perfection in these fluffy, golden little rolls infused with aromatic garlic.

INGREDIENTS

FOR THE DOUGH

1 cup (235 ml) water, lukewarm

1½ tablespoons (25 ml) extra-virgin olive oil

1 teaspoon kosher salt

3 cups (360 g) white bread flour

¼ cup (60 ml) unsweetened almond milk

2 tablespoons (7 g) instant potato flakes

2 teaspoons (8 g) instant, active dry, or bread machine yeast

1 tablespoon (7 g) garlic powder, plus extra for sprinkling

FOR THE SEASONING

¼ cup (55 g) vegan butter

2 large cloves garlic, minced

1 tablespoon (3 g) Italian seasoning

½ teaspoon kosher salt

DIRECTIONS

1. Be sure the kneading paddle is attached to the bread machine pan. Add the water, olive oil, salt, flour, nondairy milk, potato flakes, yeast, and garlic powder to the bread pan in the order listed.

2. Select the Dough setting. Press start. Line a baking sheet with parchment paper and set it aside.

3. Once the cycle is done, lightly flour a work surface. Transfer the dough to the floured surface, and sprinkle all sides of the dough with additional garlic powder.

4. Divide the dough into 12 equal pieces, and roll each piece out to a 10- to 12-inch (26- to 30-cm) rope. Shape each piece into a knot and place each knot on the baking sheet. Repeat until each rope is in a knot.

5. Cover the baking sheet loosely with plastic wrap. Let the knots rest for 30 to 45 minutes. Close to the end of the resting time, preheat your oven to 350°F (175°C).

6. Bake the knots for 15 to 20 minutes, or until lightly browned and golden.

7. Once the knots have 5 minutes left to bake, prepare the seasoning mixture: Melt the vegan butter in a small saucepan over low-medium heat. Remove the pan from the heat and stir in all the garlic, Italian seasoning, and salt.

8. Remove the garlic knots from the oven. Immediately brush them with the butter mixture.

9. Let them cool for 5 minutes. Serve them with leftover seasoning mixture or your favorite marinara.

Makes 12 knots

Vegan Pretzels

These soft and chewy treats are crafted from a simple dough mixture of water, flour, and yeast, seasoned with salt and brown sugar, then shaped into classic pretzel twists.

INGREDIENTS

3 cups (705 ml) water, lukewarm, divided

2 teaspoons (10 g) kosher salt

1 tablespoon (15 g) packed light brown sugar

3½ cups (420 g) white bread flour

2¼ teaspoons (9 g) instant, active dry, or bread machine yeast

2 tablespoons (30 g) baking soda

Coarse sea salt, for sprinkling

DIRECTIONS

1. Be sure the kneading paddle is attached to the bread machine pan. Add 1 cup (235 ml) of the water, salt, brown sugar, flour, and yeast to the bread pan in the order listed.

2. Select the Dough setting. Press start.

3. Prepare two baking sheets by lining them with parchment paper.

4. Once the dough cycle is complete, lightly flour a work surface. Transfer the dough to the floured surface, and divide it into 12 equal pieces. Roll each piece into a thin rope, shape it into a pretzel, and place the pretzels on the prepared baking sheets.

5. Cover the pretzels loosely with plastic wrap. Let them rest for 20 to 30 minutes.

6. Mix 2 cups (475 ml) of the remaining water and baking soda together in a small bowl.

7. Bring a large saucepan filled with water to a boil over high heat. Preheat your oven to 425°F (220°C).

8. After the pretzels have rested and the water is boiling, carefully boil each pretzel one at a time, flipping them halfway through for a total of 3 minutes. Drain the pretzels on a wire cooling rack, then dip each one into the baking soda solution before placing them back on the baking sheet.

9. Sprinkle coarse salt over each pretzel. Bake them in the preheated oven until they are dark and golden, about 15 to 20 minutes. Once baked, transfer the pretzels to a wire rack to cool slightly before serving.

Makes 12 pretzels

Bagels, Baby! Bagels!

Bagels are easier to make than you might think, especially when you have a bread machine. You can utilize the bread machine to effortlessly prepare the dough, followed by shaping, boiling, and baking. Take your bagels up a notch by topping them with poppy seeds, sesame seeds, or an everything seasoning blend once they're ready.

INGREDIENTS

1 cup (235 ml) warm water (110°F [43°C])

3 cups (360 g) white bread flour

2 tablespoons (26 g) organic cane sugar

1½ teaspoons kosher salt

2¼ teaspoons (9 g) instant, active dry, or bread machine yeast

1 tablespoon (9 g) cornmeal, for the baking sheet

3 tablespoons (39 g) organic cane sugar

1 tablespoon (20 g) pure maple syrup

1 tablespoon (15 ml) nondairy milk of your choice

3 tablespoons (27 g) poppy seeds

DIRECTIONS

1. Be sure the kneading paddle is attached to your bread machine pan. Combine water, flour, sugar, salt, and yeast in the bread pan in the order listed.

2. Select the Dough setting, and remove the dough after about 90 minutes.

3. Lightly flour a work surface. Transfer the dough to the floured surface and allow it to rest for 10 to 15 minutes.

4. Divide the dough into nine equal portions. Shape each into a small ball, flatten into a circle, and use your thumb to create a hole in the center. Twirl the circle to enlarge the hole and even out the dough.

5. Place the bagels back on the floured surface. Cover them with a clean tea towel, and let rest for another 10 minutes.

6. While the dough rests, bring 3 quarts (2.8 L) of water to a boil in a large pot. Preheat your oven to 375°F (190°C) and sprinkle cornmeal on an ungreased baking sheet.

7. Add the sugar to the boiling water. Carefully boil two bagels at a time for 1 minute each, turning halfway through. Briefly drain on a clean tea towel, then arrange the bagels on the prepared baking sheet. Repeat until all the bagels are on the baking sheet.

8. Mix the maple syrup and nondairy milk together in a small bowl. Brush each bagel with the wash, and sprinkle with poppy seeds.

9. Bake the bagels in the preheated oven until golden brown, about 20 to 25 minutes.

Makes 9 bagels

Bread Machine Pizza Dough

Simple, delectable, and incredibly versatile—pizza dough is nearly effortless to make in your bread machine. This recipe will make you a master pizza-maker.

INGREDIENTS

1 cup (235 ml) water, lukewarm

1 teaspoon pure maple syrup

1½ teaspoons kosher salt

1½ tablespoons (25 ml) extra-virgin olive oil

3⅓ cups (410 g) white bread flour

1¾ teaspoons instant, active dry, or bread machine yeast

DIRECTIONS

1. Be sure the kneading paddle is attached to your bread machine pan. Add the water, maple syrup, salt, olive oil, flour, and yeast to the bread pan in the order listed.

2. Select the Dough setting. Press start.

3. Once the cycle is finished, remove the dough. Use it immediately to create your favorite pizza pie. You can also wrap the dough in plastic wrap and store it in the fridge for up to 3 days.

Makes one 20- to 24-inch (51 to 61 cm) large round pizza or two smaller 10- to 12-inch (25 to 30 cm) small round pizzas

CHAPTER

6

SWEET BREADS AND CHOCOLATE BREADS

If you think bread machines are just for savory loaves, think again! This chapter explores the sweeter side of breadmaking with recipes for everything from moist banana breads to rich babka. Indulge your sweet tooth with ooey-gooey cinnamon bread, a tangy lemon loaf, and more—all made easily in your bread machine. These decadent treats are perfect for breakfast, dessert, or anytime you need a little something sweet.

Holiday Panettone Loaf

I'm a little embarrassed I had never heard of this type of bread until doing the research for this book. But, after making it I was hooked. Scrap the crappy fruitcake your Aunt Jane gives you every year and make this instead.

INGREDIENTS

½ cup (120 ml) unsweetened almond milk, lukewarm

¼ cup (55 g) vegan butter, room temperature, cut into ½-inch (1-cm) pieces

½ cup (120 ml) aquafaba (see page 20)

½ teaspoon kosher salt

¼ cup (50 g) organic cane sugar

2¾ cups (344 g) organic unbleached all-purpose flour

1 tablespoon (6 g) orange zest

¾ teaspoon ground nutmeg

2 teaspoons (8 g) instant, active dry, or bread machine yeast

¾ cup (weigh varies) dried fruit mixture (e.g., raisins, cherries)

DIRECTIONS

1. Attach the kneading paddle to the bread machine pan. Add the nondairy milk, vegan butter, aquafaba, salt, sugar, flour, orange zest, nutmeg, and yeast to the bread pan in the order listed.

2. Select the Sweet or Rapid setting on your bread machine. Choose the 1½-pound (680-g) loaf size. Press start.

3. When the Add-In signal sounds, add the dried fruit.

4. Once the bread is finished, remove it from the bread machine. Transfer it to a wire rack to cool. Once the bread is at room temperature, slice and enjoy!

Makes one 1½-pound (680-g) loaf

Decadent Chocolate Bread

This cocoa bread has a moist texture and rich chocolatey flavor, and it is insanely delicious. Add a scoop of vegan vanilla ice cream to make it a great dessert, or enjoy it with fresh fruit for a satisfying kid-friendly breakfast.

INGREDIENTS

1 cup (235 ml) unsweetened soymilk, warmed

3 tablespoons (45 ml) aquafaba (see page 20)

¼ cup (55 g) vegan butter, softened

1 teaspoon pure vanilla extract

3 cups (360 g) white bread flour

¼ cup (60 g) dark brown sugar, packed

¼ cup (22 g) unsweetened cocoa powder

2¼ teaspoons (9 g) instant, active dry, or bread machine yeast

DIRECTIONS

1. Be sure the kneading paddle is attached to your bread machine pan. Add the soymilk, aquafaba, vegan butter, vanilla, flour, brown sugar, coca powder, and yeast to the bread pan in the order listed.

2. Select the Rapid or Sweet setting. Choose the 2-pound (907-g) loaf size. Press start.

3. Once the bread has finished baking, remove it from the machine. Allow it to cool for several minutes.

4. Slice, serve, and enjoy! Use plastic wrap on any leftovers, and store them at room temperature for 3 to 4 days.

Makes one 2-pound (907-g) loaf

Cherry Chocolate Bread

The bursts of tartness from the cherries perfectly complement the deep, indulgent notes of dark chocolate in this rich and decadent bread.

INGREDIENTS

½ cup (120 ml) unsweetened almond milk, lukewarm

¼ cup (55 g) vegan butter, softened, cut into ½-inch (1-cm) pieces

½ cup (120 ml) aquafaba (see page 20)

1 teaspoon kosher salt

¼ cup (50 g) organic cane sugar

3 cups (375 g) organic unbleached all-purpose flour

1¾ teaspoons instant, active dry, or bread machine yeast

⅔ cup (116 g) vegan dark chocolate chunks or chocolate chips

½ cup (70 g) dried cherries (see note)

DIRECTIONS

1. Attach the kneading paddle to the bread machine pan. Add the nondairy milk, vegan butter, aquafaba, salt, sugar, flour, and yeast to the bread pan in the order listed.

2. Select the Sweet setting or equivalent on your bread machine. Select the desired crust color (if available) and the 1½-pound (608-g) loaf size. Press start.

3. Once the paddle signal sounds, pause the bread machine. Lightly flour a work surface. Remove the dough and kneading paddle.

4. Place the dough on the floured surface. Roll it into a rectangle 14 to 16 inches (36 to 41 cm) long and ¼ inch (6 mm) thick.

5. Evenly spread the chocolate and cherries over the dough. Roll the dough into a tight log shape and tuck the ends on each side to seal it.

6. Place the dough back into the bread pan. Be sure the kneading paddle is out. Press start to restart the machine.

7. Once the bread is finished, remove it from the pan to cool completely. Then slice and enjoy.

Makes one 1½-pound (680-g) loaf

Note: You can use another dried fruit in place of the cherries if you like. A few of my favorites are cranberries, raisins, apricots, and even prunes.

Chocolate Sour Cream Bread

This decadent bread combines the deep, cocoa-infused taste of chocolate with the tangy creaminess of dairy-free sour cream in a moist and tender loaf. It works as a satisfying breakfast option or a delectable dessert for later in the day.

INGREDIENTS

½ cup plus 1 tablespoon (135 ml) unsweetened almond milk, lukewarm

½ cup (115 g) vegan sour cream

½ cup (115 g) unsweetened plain vegan yogurt

1 teaspoon pure vanilla extract

½ cup (100 g) organic cane sugar

⅓ cup (75 g) packed light brown sugar

1⅓ cups (167 g) organic unbleached all-purpose flour

¼ cup (22 g) unsweetened cocoa powder

¾ teaspoon baking powder

½ teaspoon baking soda

½ teaspoon kosher salt

¾ cup (131 g) vegan chocolate chips

⅓ cup (37 g) chopped pecans

DIRECTIONS

1. Make sure the kneading paddle is attached to your bread machine pan. Spray the inside of the bread pan with cooking spray.

2. Add the nondairy milk, vegan sour cream, vegan yogurt, vanilla, sugar, brown sugar, flour, cocoa powder, baking powder, baking soda, salt, chocolate chips, and pecans to the bread pan in the order listed.

3. Select the Cake setting and the 2-pound (907-g) loaf size. Press start. Scrape down the sides with a rubber spatula while the batter is mixing. This will ensure all the ingredients are fully incorporated. Once they are incorporated, you can stop and allow the machine to continue.

4. Once the cycle has finished, remove the bread from the machine. Transfer it to a wire rack, and allow the bread to cool before slicing.

Makes one 2-pound (907-g) loaf

Bread Machine Babka

This sumptuous treat features a blend of a rich chocolate and cinnamon filling delicately swirled within a soft, pillowy dough.

INGREDIENTS

FOR THE DOUGH

⅔ cup (160 ml) unsweetened almond milk

¼ cup (55 g) vegan butter, room temperature, cut into ½-inch (1-cm) pieces

½ cup (120 ml) aquafaba (see page 20)

1½ teaspoons pure vanilla extract

¼ cup (50 g) organic cane sugar

1 teaspoon kosher salt

3 cups (375 g) organic unbleached all-purpose flour

¼ teaspoon ground nutmeg

2 teaspoons (8 g) instant, active dry, or bread machine yeast

FOR THE FILLING

¼ cup (50 g) organic cane sugar

1 tablespoon (7 g) ground cinnamon

1½ tablespoons (8 g) unsweetened cocoa powder

Pinch of salt

FOR THE GLAZE

1 cup (120 g) confectioners' sugar

1–2 tablespoons (15–30 ml) almond milk or nondairy milk of your choice, plus more if needed

1 teaspoon pure vanilla extract

continued >

Bread Machine Babka

continued

DIRECTIONS

1. Attach the kneading paddle to the bread machine pan. Add the nondairy milk, vegan butter, aquafaba, vanilla, sugar, salt, flour, nutmeg, and yeast to the bread pan in the order listed.

2. Select the Sweet setting. Choose the desired crust color (if available) and choose the 1½-pound (608-g) loaf size. Press start.

3. While the dough is being prepared, go ahead and make the filling: Place the sugar, cinnamon, cocoa powder, and salt in a small bowl. Whisk together to combine. Set it aside.

4. Once the paddle signal sounds, pause your bread machine. Remove the dough and the kneading paddle. Lightly flour a work surface.

5. Place the dough on the floured surface and roll it out to about 14 to 16 inches (36 to 41 cm) long and ¼ inch (6 mm) thick, then evenly sprinkle the filling mixture over the dough. Starting at the short end of the dough, roll it up into a tight log shape. Tuck and squeeze the ends to seal it.

6. Place the dough back into the bread pan. Remember to make sure the kneading paddle is removed. Restart the machine.

7. When the bread only has about 5 minutes left to bake, make the glaze: Combine the confectioners' sugar, nondairy milk, and vanilla in a small bowl. Whisk until it is smooth. Add a little more liquid if needed until you get the consistency you want.

8. Once the bread has finished baking, remove it from the bread pan. Transfer it to a wire rack, and immediately cover the babka with glaze. Let the babka cool completely, then slice it and enjoy!

Makes one 1½-pound (680-g) loaf

Bread Machine Banana Nut Bread

This bread combines the irresistible sweetness of ripe bananas with the rich crunch of chopped nuts. The automated precision of the bread machine ensures a consistently tender texture that practically melts in your mouth with each bite.

INGREDIENTS

½ cup (112 g) vegan butter, softened

⅔ cup (160 ml) unsweetened soymilk or unsweetened almond milk

2 tablespoons (14 g) ground flaxseed plus 3 tablespoons (45 ml) water

2½ cups (314 g) organic unbleached all-purpose flour

1 cup (200 g) organic cane sugar

1½ tablespoons (21 g) baking powder

½ teaspoon baking soda

1 teaspoon kosher salt

⅔ cup (150 g) very ripe mashed bananas

½ cup (60 g) chopped walnuts

DIRECTIONS

1. Be sure the kneading paddle is attached to your bread machine pan. Lightly coat the bread machine pan with cooking spray, making sure the entire area is covered.

2. Add the butter, nondairy milk, flaxseed, flour, sugar, baking powder, baking soda, salt, bananas, and walnuts in the order they are listed to a mixing bowl. Stir to combine. Pour the mixture into the bread machine pan.

3. Select the Quick Bread or Cake setting. Choose the 2-pound (907-g) loaf size. Press start. Check after a minute to make sure the mixture is well combined.

4. Let the banana bread cook until the cycle has finished. Remove the pan from the machine. Let the banana bread completely cool before removing it from the bread pan and slicing.

Makes one 2-pound (907-g) loaf

Vegan Banana Chocolate Chip Walnut Bread

Nuts, fruit, and chocolate—what more could you ask for? I eat this bread at breakfast sometimes, or with vegan vanilla ice cream alongside for dessert at dinnertime.

INGREDIENTS

½ cup (120 ml) unsweetened almond milk, lukewarm

1½ teaspoons vinegar

½ cup (112 g) vegan butter, room temperature, cut into ½-inch (1-cm) pieces

½ cup (120 ml) aquafaba (see page 20)

1 teaspoon pure vanilla extract

3 medium-size ripe bananas, mashed

½ teaspoon kosher salt

1 cup (200 g) organic cane sugar

2 cups (250 g) organic unbleached all-purpose flour

1 teaspoon baking soda

¾ teaspoon baking powder

⅔ cup (80 g) chopped walnuts

¼ cup (44 g) vegan chocolate chips

DIRECTIONS

1. Be sure the kneading paddle is attached to the bread pan. Spray the bread pan with cooking spray.

2. Whisk together the nondairy milk and the vinegar in a small bowl. Let it sit to curdle. Then, add the mixture, vegan butter, aquafaba, vanilla, bananas, salt, sugar, flour, baking soda, baking powder, walnuts, and chocolate chips to the bread pan in the order listed.

3. Select the Cake setting. Choose the 2-pound (907-g) loaf size. Press start. Scrape down the sides with a rubber spatula while the batter is mixing. This will ensure all the ingredients are fully incorporated. Once they are incorporated, you can stop and allow the machine to continue.

4. Once the cycle has finished, remove the bread from the bread pan. Allow it to completely cool on a wire rack before slicing.

Makes one 2-pound (907-g) loaf

Bread Machine Vegan Pound Cake

Although bread machines excel at yeast breads, they are also very good at making yeastless quick breads and simple cake-like batters, as in this recipe. Prepare to be amazed by the sheer decadence of vegan bread machine pound cake! With its moist crumb and rich flavor, this plant-powered delight proves that you don't need eggs or dairy to indulge in a slice of pure bliss. So, let your bread machine do the work while you sit back and savor every heavenly bite of this cruelty-free confection.

INGREDIENTS

⅓ cup (80 ml) unsweetened almond milk, lukewarm

¾ cup (175 ml) aquafaba (see page 20)

½ cup (112 g) vegan butter, melted

1 teaspoon pure vanilla extract

1 tablespoon (14 g) baking powder

2 cups (250 g) white bread flour

1 cup (200 g) organic cane sugar

DIRECTIONS

1. Be sure the kneading paddle is attached to your bread machine pan. Add the nondairy milk, aquafaba, vegan butter, vanilla, baking powder, flour, and sugar to the bread pan in the order listed.

2. Select the Cake setting. Choose medium crust color (if available) and the 2-pound (907-g) loaf size. Press start.

3. Once the cycle has finished, remove the cake from the bread pan. Transfer it to a wire rack, and let it cool for 5 to 10 minutes before serving.

Makes one 2-pound (907-g) loaf

Vegan Bread Machine Cinnamon Swirl Bread

Toast this bread for breakfast for a sweet indulgence. It is less sugary than a cinnamon roll or other pastry.

INGREDIENTS

1¼ cups (295 ml) unsweetened soymilk, room temperature

2½ tablespoons (35 g) vegan butter, room temperature, cut into ½-inch (1-cm) pieces

¼ cup (60 ml) aquafaba (see page 20)

1 teaspoon kosher salt

2 tablespoons (26 g) organic cane sugar

4 cups (500 g) organic unbleached all-purpose flour

2 teaspoons (8 g) instant, active dry, or bread machine yeast

FOR THE CINNAMON SWIRL

⅓ cup (66 g) organic cane sugar

3 tablespoons (21 g) ground cinnamon

DIRECTIONS

1. Attach the kneading paddle to the bread machine pan. Add the soymilk, vegan butter, aquafaba, salt, sugar, flour, and yeast to the bread pan in the order listed.

2. Select the Basic or White setting. Choose the desired crust color (if available), and select 2-pound (907-g) loaf size. Press start.

3. While the dough is mixing, make the cinnamon swirl: Combine the sugar and cinnamon in a small bowl. Set it aside. Lightly flour a clean work surface for rolling.

4. When the Add-In signal sounds, pause the unit. Remove the dough and place it on the floured surface. Roll the dough into a rectangle that is 14 to 16 inches (36 to 41 cm) long and about ¼ inch (6 mm) thick.

5. Sprinkle the cinnamon swirl mixture over the entire surface of the dough.

6. Start with the short side and roll the dough into a tight cylinder. Tuck the ends underneath to seal the dough.

7. Remove the kneading paddle. Fit the dough back into the bread pan. Press start to continue making the bread.

8. Once the bread has finished baking, remove it from the machine. Let it cool completely on a wire rack before slicing.

Makes one 2-pound (907-g) loaf

Vegan Lemon Cake Bread

I used to love Starbucks lemon loaf, but it's not vegan. I am vegan, so there's that. But this vegan bread machine lemon bread totally fills that void—and even beyond. This sweet bread is perfect for your little tea party or slicing off a big hunk and shoving it down your gullet . . . as I like to do. And, the bread machine makes it stupid simple to create.

INGREDIENTS

FOR THE BREAD

½ cup (120 ml) unsweetened almond milk, lukewarm

½ cup (112 g) vegan butter, melted

½ cup (120 ml) aquafaba (see page 20)

1 cup (200 g) organic cane sugar

⅛ teaspoon kosher salt

2 tablespoons (28 ml) lemon juice

1 teaspoon baking powder

1½ cups (188 g) organic unbleached all-purpose flour

1 tablespoon (6 g) grated lemon peel

FOR THE GLAZE

½ cup (60 g) confectioners' sugar

2 tablespoons (28 ml) lemon juice

DIRECTIONS

1. Make sure the kneading paddle is attached to the bread machine pan. Add the nondairy milk, vegan butter, aquafaba, sugar, salt, lemon juice, baking powder, flour, and lemon peel to the bread pan in the order listed.

2. Choose the Cake setting. Select the 2-pound (907-g) loaf size. Press start.

3. Once the cycle has finished, remove the bread from the pan. Transfer it to a wire rack.

4. To make the glaze: Stir together the confectioners' sugar and lemon juice in a small bowl. Drizzle the glaze over the lemon bread.

5. Let the bread rest for 10 minutes, then slice and serve.

Makes one 2-pound (907-g) loaf

Big Bear Claws from the Bread Machine

These pastries have a perfect flaky texture that captures the essence of traditional bear claws, but catering to a plant-based palate.

INGREDIENTS

FOR THE DOUGH

¼ cup (60 ml) water, cool

¼ cup (60 g) vegan sour cream, cool

¼ cup (50 g) organic cane sugar

½ teaspoon kosher salt

1 flax egg (see note) or vegan egg replacement

¼ cup (55 g) vegan butter, room temperature, cut into ½-inch (1-cm) pieces

2¼ cups plus 1 tablespoon (290 g) organic unbleached all-purpose flour

2 teaspoons (8 g) instant, active dry, or bread machine yeast

FOR THE FILLING

2 tablespoons (28 g) vegan butter, softened

¼ cup (50 g) organic cane sugar

1 teaspoon ground cinnamon

FOR THE FROSTING

1 tablespoon (14 g) vegan butter

1 tablespoon (15 g) vegan cream cheese

1½ tablespoons (25 ml) almond milk

1 cup (120 g) confectioners' sugar

¼ cup (28 g) toasted sliced almonds

DIRECTIONS

1. To make the dough: Be sure the kneading paddle is attached to your bread machine pan. Add the water, vegan sour cream, sugar, salt, flax egg, vegan butter, flour, and yeast to the bread pan in the order listed.

2. Choose the Dough setting. Press start. Check the dough twice during mixing and kneading: Ensure the paddles are engaged correctly after the machine starts. Check the dough's consistency 15 minutes into the cycle; it should stick to the sides and pull away cleanly. Adjust the dough's wetness by adding flour or liquid 1 tablespoon at a time.

3. After the cycle completes, proceed if the dough has doubled. If not, wait until it does before moving on.

4. When the dough has doubled in size, grease a baking sheet. Lightly flour a work surface. Roll the dough out on the floured surface into a 6- × 24-inch (15- × 60-cm) rectangle.

5. Fill the roll by spreading the softened vegan butter on the rectangle. Then, mix the sugar and cinnamon in a small bowl to combine. Sprinkle the mixture evenly over the rectangle.

6. Roll it up tightly, then slice it into ten pieces.

7. Make two cuts into each slice using kitchen shears or a pizza cutter, twisting each slice slightly. Place them on the baking sheet.

8. Cover them with a tea towel, and let them rise until almost doubled, about 45 minutes to 1 hour. Preheat your oven to 375°F (190°C) close to the end of the rising time.

9. Bake the bear claws for 15 to 20 minutes, or until golden brown.

10. While the rolls bake, make the frosting: Soften the vegan butter and vegan cream cheese. Combine them with the almond milk in a bowl, and beat the frosting ingredients until smooth. Add the confectioners' sugar and mix until smooth.

11. When the bear claws finish baking, drizzle the frosting over them with a spoon or use a small plastic bag with a corner cut off to pipe the frosting.

12. Sprinkle them with the toasted sliced almonds immediately before the frosting dries or press the frosted rolls into a plate of almonds.

Makes 10 bear claws

Note: To make the flax egg: In a small bowl, add 2½ tablespoons (38 ml) of warm water plus 1 tablespoon (7 g) of ground flaxseed. Stir until well combined, and let it sit for 10 minutes. Makes 1 flax egg.

LET'S MAKE SOME JAM

While primarily used for baking bread, your versatile machine can also whip up luscious jams and preserves. This chapter guides you through simple recipes to capture the bright, ripe flavors of fresh fruits. From classic raspberry and mixed berry jams to unique lemon blueberry and pear preserves, you'll learn just how easy it is to make spreads that taste like summertime year-round. Slather them on breads, scones, or simply enjoy by the spoonful!

Lemon Blueberry Jam

Bursting with sweet, juicy blueberries and a bright citrus punch, this lemon blueberry jam is sunshine in a jar. The tart lemon complements the blueberries perfectly for a vibrant, well-balanced flavor. Best of all, it comes together quickly with just a few simple ingredients in your trusty bread machine.

INGREDIENTS

6 cups (870 g) fresh blueberries

1¼ cups (250 g) organic cane sugar

1 tablespoon (9 g) powdered pectin

¼ cup (60 ml) fresh lemon juice

1 teaspoon lemon zest

Pinch of salt

DIRECTIONS

1. Make sure the kneading paddle is attached to the bread machine pan. Add the blueberries, sugar, pectin, lemon juice, lemon zest, and salt to the bread pan in the order listed.

2. Select the Jam setting. Press start.

3. Use a rubber spatula to scrape the pan about 10 minutes after the machine has started.

4. Once the cycle has finished, spoon your jam into clean, dry jars. Wait for the jam to completely cool before attaching lids.

5. You can store the jam in your refrigerator for up to 3 weeks.

Makes about 6 cups (1.9 kg)

Raspberry Jam

This gorgeous ruby-red raspberry jam is a work of art and deliciousness. Tart and sweet with an intense raspberry flavor, it's the perfect way to capture the taste of fresh berries at their peak. Making it in the bread machine is virtually effortless—just a few ingredients and your machine does the work for you.

INGREDIENTS

3 cups (375 g) fresh raspberries

¾ cup (150 g) organic cane sugar

1 tablespoon (15 ml) lemon juice

1 teaspoon powdered pectin

DIRECTIONS

1. First, softly mash the raspberries in a bowl.

2. Make sure the kneading paddle is attached to the bread machine pan. Add the raspberries, sugar, lemon juice, and pectin to the bread pan in the order listed.

3. Select the Jam setting. Press start.

4. Use a rubber spatula to scrape the pan about 10 minutes after the machine has started.

5. Once the cycle has finished, pour the jam into clean, dry jars. Let them cool before attaching the lids.

6. Store the jam in the refrigerator for up to 3 weeks.

Makes about 3 cups (960 g)

Mixed Berry Jam

A colorful medley of raspberries, blueberries, and strawberries blend together in this luscious mixed berry jam. It has a lovely mixed berry flavor with the perfect balance of sweetness and tartness. Whip up a batch effortlessly in your bread machine for a taste of summer you can enjoy all year long.

INGREDIENTS

4 cups (580 g) fresh strawberries, quartered

2 cups (250 g) fresh raspberries

2 cups (290 g) fresh blueberries

1 cup (200 g) organic cane sugar

1 tablespoon (9 g) powdered pectin

DIRECTIONS

1. Make sure the kneading paddle is attached to the bread machine pan. Add the strawberries, raspberries, blueberries, sugar, and pectin to the bread pan in the order listed.

2. Select the Jam setting. Press start.

3. For optimal mixing, scrape the pan about 10 to 15 minutes after the program commences.

4. Once the cycle has finished, transfer the jam to clean, dry jars. Allow them to completely cool before attaching the lids.

5. Store the jam in the refrigerator for up to 3 weeks.

Makes about 4 cups (1.2 kg)

Pear Preserves

These luscious pear preserves let the delicate flavor of fresh pears shine. They have a luxuriously smooth, spreadable texture. Making them in the bread machine is easy—just a few simple ingredients for a taste of fall you can enjoy anytime. Spoon some over oatmeal, yogurt, or warm-from-the-oven bread and let the pear perfection transport your senses.

INGREDIENTS

4 large pears, peeled, cored, and diced (about 1¾ lbs. [794 g])

1 cup (200 g) organic cane sugar

¼ cup (27 g) powdered pectin

1 tablespoon (15 ml) fresh lemon juice

Pinch of salt

DIRECTIONS

1. Make sure the kneading paddle is attached to the bread machine pan. Add the pears, sugar, pectin, lemon juice, and salt to the bread pan in the order listed.

2. Select the Jam setting. Press start.

3. For optimal mixing, scrape the pan about 10 to 15 minutes after the program commences.

4. Once the cycle has finished, transfer the jam to clean, dry jars. Allow them to completely cool before attaching the lids.

5. Store the jam in the refrigerator for up to 3 weeks.

Makes about 4 cups (1.2 kg)

Some Bonus Tips and Tricks

ENHANCING TEXTURE AND FLAVOR IN BREAD MACHINE BAKING

Optimize the texture and flavor of your bread machine loaves by fine-tuning your recipes. Try using different types of flour, such as whole-wheat or rye, to achieve varying levels of texture and taste. Adding vital wheat gluten can enhance the elasticity of the dough, resulting in a lighter, airier crumb. Experiment with incorporating flavor boosters such as herbs, spices, or even garlic and onion powder to infuse your bread with extra depth and complexity.

CUSTOMIZING BREAD MACHINE RECIPES TO YOUR TASTE

Tailor bread machine recipes to suit your personal preferences and dietary requirements. Adjust the amount of sugar or salt to your liking, or swap out ingredients that you know are going to take your creation up another notch. You can also experiment with different types of sweeteners, such as honey or maple syrup, for a unique flavor twist. Don't forget to explore specialty flour blends and alternative grains for added variety in your bread repertoire.

STORING AND FREEZING YOUR FRESHLY BAKED BREAD MACHINE CREATIONS

Preserve the freshness of your bread machine creations by storing them properly. Once cooled, wrap your loaf tightly in plastic wrap or aluminum foil to maintain moisture and prevent staleness. For longer storage, slice the bread and freeze individual portions in freezer bags or containers. When ready to enjoy, simply thaw slices at room temperature or reheat them in the oven for a warm, just-baked taste. With these storage techniques, you can enjoy your homemade bread machine bread for days or even weeks after baking.

ABOUT THE AUTHOR

Shane Martin is the cook, writer, and photographer behind the blog *Shane & Simple*, where his mission is to create and share recipes that are, as he writes, "straight-up easy, delicious, plant-based, and vegan," and where a number of bread recipes have been featured. He founded the blog in 2018 as he took time off from a successful career in Nashville as a songwriter for Sony Records in order to address obesity and other health concerns, which he successfully conquered via a new vegan diet. His work has been featured on the cover of *VEGWORLD* magazine, in the UK's top vegan magazine *Vegan Life*, in *Forbes*, and on *Bored Panda* as well as on the *Plantstrong Podcast* with Rip Esselstyn. He is the primary daily cook in the home he shares with his wife and five children in Booneville, Mississippi, to which they have relocated from Nashville.

ACKNOWLEDGMENTS

No book is written in a vacuum, and this one is no exception. While I will undoubtedly fail to mention everyone who deserves thanks, I will do my best to acknowledge those who played a role in making this work possible. From the bottom of my heart, thank you so much to the following.

The incredible team at Quarto and Harvard Common Press. It amazes me to see how a book goes from nothing to beautiful—I stand amazed. You have allowed me to be a part of not just one, but two books, and I could not be more grateful for the experience. Dan, Anne, John, Jenna, and everyone else who painstakingly and patiently walked me through this experience, "thank you" is not a big enough expression. It's been an honor.

Chef AJ. Everyone says you should never meet your heroes because you might be disappointed, but that does not apply to you. Thank you for your support this last year! (I still can't believe I have your number and can text you. Let's do a waterslide soon!)

Rip Esselstyn. Thank you for being the motivation that got me started on this plant-based journey almost twelve years ago. It saved my life.

Jason and Mary Ann. Thank you for your support and prayers, and for letting us live with you for six weeks when we moved back to town. Fun times, eh? Mary Ann, thanks for the loan of props for my first book. (I brought everything back, right?)

Trey Lambert. Thank you for your friendship, sense of humor, and eventually believing I have a real job. Be sure and tell Clayton "hello."

My children: Maddie (and Justin, your husband), Jonathan, Macy, Mackenzie, and Millie-Jane. Thank you for the life you've given your mother and me. I love you all more than you could ever possibly imagine.

Andrea. Thank you for loving me and always being there. Our story has been anything but normal, and I wouldn't change one thing. I love you!

INDEX

Enjoy!